"'By sharing, we belong, and by belonging we can share.' In this memoir, Theo does not hold back. Her vulnerability is palpable on every page. I found nuggets of wisdom in every chapter and have my annotations to prove it. With her words, I laughed, I cried, and I found my own healing as I remembered walking through grief in my own life. I hope others who read this book experience the same. As the title suggests, no two people grieve the same way. Yet I find it interesting how in reading one's account of their grief, another can find healing. Their experiences are not the same, yet they have a connection. I think that's beautiful."

—**Ashley Teague**, Former Colleague, High School
English and Creative Writing Teacher

"Even though Theo's book exposes the many layers of grief, there is a beautiful and unique love story at the foundation of this memoir. Her authentic recollections are written in such a way that you can truly feel the emotions in your own heart. This book made me laugh. It made me cry. It gave me comfort in knowing that I wasn't alone in my own roller-coaster of grief-driven emotions. It gave me a sense of understanding, not only my own feelings and actions during my time of grief, but the way others respond to grief as well. It gave me hope that acceptance and healing is possible."

—**Kristi Hiland**, Elementary Teacher, Life Organizer

Praise for *My Grief Is Not Like Yours*

"When I read the book and heard her voice, it was like I was hearing the lyrics to a Grammy Award-winning song. Her country 'voice' turns these heavy topics into an uplifting, hope-filled testimonial. She invites us to join in the revelations as she helps us know we can feel love and light after grief. We can do it!"

—**Jackie Waldman**, Author and Speaker, *The Courage to Give*

"Theo's journey reminds us all that life is not fair. It can be very hard, but we have to go on because we must. Many of us have lost our parents to the inevitability of death, but not the way Theo did. Her mother dies in a tragic farm accident, her marriage crumbles, and then her dad ends his life. I love Theo's story because I love Theo. And how can you not love someone who loves their dog?"

—**Dale Hansen**, American Sports Commentato
Writer, Speaker, and Influenc

"Theo is so honest with us that sometimes I almost didn't w her to be because the details were so unimaginable. H ever, without each descriptive picture that she paints, the wouldn't be genuine and true. If there is anything that Th it's *true*. Joe Bob, Sue, and the Lord prepared Theo for th that she was to be dealt. The lessons she learned from her showed her how to live and love well . . . show up, be pre others even when it's yucky, even when *we* are the yuck wait to meet Sue and Joe Bob when I get to Heaven! I the Lord lets Sue fix us some peanut brittle, and I bet growing the peanuts."

—**Linda Davis**, Grammy Awa
Singer, Songwriter, and

"Like grief, agriculture is unique to each farm and culture has major stresses and risks both moneta cally. She shares her story of her family's farm a effects of grief and stress afterward. It takes great up and share such a personal journey as Theo ha will encourage others to be able to share and as

—**John Paul Dineen**, I
Agricul

MY GRIEF IS NOT LIKE YOURS

MY GRIEF IS NOT LIKE YOURS

LEARNING TO LIVE AFTER UNIMAGINABLE LOSS, A DAUGHTER'S JOURNEY

THEO BOYD

Theo Boyd

2024

Forefront
BOOKS

My Grief Is Not Like Yours: Learning to Live after Unimaginable Loss, a Daughter's Journey
Copyright © 2023 by Theo Boyd

Published by Forefront Books.
Distributed by Simon & Schuster.

Library of Congress Control Number: 2023901454

Print ISBN: 978-1637631560
E-book ISBN: 978-1637631577
Cover Design by Bruce Gore, Gore Studio, Inc.
Interior Design by PerfecType, Nashville, TN

Scripture quotations are taken from the King James version of the Bible. Public domain.

DEDICATIONS

*Dedicated to a creation so incomprehensible
that I am left with only a beautiful mystery
who was my host—my mother.
Her life, miraculous.
Her love, boundless.
Her spirit, eternal.*

*And to my father, who joined this book
on Father's Day 2022.
His life, empowering.
His love, intense.
His spirit, joined with hers.*

And to my Manly,

Each time I read this book, I picture you—
lying at my feet, waiting on the occasional crumb to fall.

This book only happened because of
you, my one true constant.
You never left my side, my feet, my heart.
You laid beside me when I cried.
You laid beside Daddy when he cried.
You offered comfort to all the animals on the farm,
even though some of them seemed annoyed.

When writing this book, you listened. You approved.
My dog, my friend, my love—my Manly.

TO THE PEOPLE AND PLACES

Shantana (Shan),

God knew this book needed your touch. With each chapter, I eagerly awaited your compassionate feedback and keen insight into the reader's mind. In the difficult moments working through the harder memories, you listened and endured with me, helping me transfer the emotions into words. When I was stressing over deadlines and "techy" stuff, you brought a calmness to the room that allowed the words to flow. Without you, this book, this story, this mission would not have felt complete. You are an angel placed in my life to help me have the strength and clarity to share my journey. I am thankful for you, not only as the best beta reader on the planet, but as a person I call my friend.

Megan & Allison,

Having your advice, suggestions, corrections, and most of all, your love during this time meant more to me than words on a page will ever be able to say. You listened and supported me with your wisdom through this process, you have helped make this book a reality. Thank you, my sweet friends.

Setting is crucial. For me, the setting for writing this book happened in two places.

Overflow Coffee Company,

As a child, I would come into this building to pick up a JCPenney order from the pharmacy counter in the back. My memories here are as warm as the coffee that I now drink inside. Thank you for hosting me during those long days of writing upstairs and for allowing me a space all to myself. Your "Spilling Bee" and tomato basil soup kept the words flowing.

Hillsboro City Library,

During the summer months, Momma would take me to the library to check out books. The smell, the warmth, the escape from sound all contributed to my ability to recount what was needed for this book. I think you are the best kept secret—a free space, free Internet, and resources at your fingertips. I never dreamed I would return to this building of books many years later to actually write one. Thank you for being there for me, then and now.

CONTENTS

Introduction 17

Chapter 1   Sue. 23
Chapter 2   Chocolate-Covered Strawberries. 33
Chapter 3   What the Fuck?. 59
Chapter 4   What Is Grief Anyway? 77
Chapter 5   The Ring 87
Chapter 6   Joe. .99
Chapter 7   Peanut Shells 109
Chapter 8   Clouds 131
Chapter 9   Mr. Fine. 147
Chapter 10   The Final Goodbyes 161
Chapter 11   More "F" Words 179
Chapter 12   The "D" Diets: Death, Divorce,
             and Discovery. 201
Chapter 13   In the Room. 217

SPECIAL EXTRAS

A Remembrance Exercise. 223

Remembering Her .233

"What She Hears": A Poem 237

Remembering Him .239

"582-9307": A Poem 250

"Proud to be a Peanut Farmer's Daughter" 251

Resources. 255

No More Someday .259

Momma's Recipes. 261

"50 Shadows": Theo's First-Place
  Award-Winning Essay. 267

CONTENT NOTE

Some of the material in this book may be difficult to read or listen to. This story contains detailed information and raw emotion surrounding a tragic farm accident and a suicide. This may bring emotions and memories to the surface or create a feeling of discomfort to the reader. Please be mindful of your mental health while reading about my journey.

INTRODUCTION

This is the core of the human spirit . . .
If we can find something to live for—if we can
find some meaning to put at the center of our lives—
even the worst kind of suffering becomes bearable.
—Viktor Frankl

In June 2019, I had it all.

I was teaching high school English, had a successful husband, and loving, supportive parents. We were happy, and life was moving along routinely. I remember sitting out by our pool one evening at our beautiful home in the country, being thankful for all that God had blessed me with. My daughter was away at college, and life had become what I had always wanted—enjoyable, happy, and fulfilling.

It was. Until July 29, 2019.

That is the day that started a contagion of unexpected and tragic events that would leave me without hope, without purpose, without direction. I was like a peanut shell left out in a foggy field, a recipe missing some of its ingredients. I was learning to play a new life song and not able to hit all the right notes.

When I started writing this book three years ago, I never realized the twists and turns it would take. From the moment I realized my world would never be the same, I had to record my thoughts, questions, feelings, and fears. I wanted to write down what I couldn't seem to find in other books. I needed to read something that hit me as hard as I had been hit. I was desperately looking for my purpose. I had forgotten what hope was. My whole life had changed. *Who was I now?* I didn't realize it at the time, but I was learning to live all over again.

The three tragic events that happened over the past three years would bring most to their knees, and it did, for a time. Momma was unexpectedly killed on the farm. My husband began to go outside of our marriage for comfort during our time of grief, and Daddy ended his life from the pain of it all. But as Viktor Frankl says in *Man's Search for Meaning*: "Everything can be taken from a man or woman but one thing: the last of the human freedoms—to choose one's attitude in any given set of circumstances, to choose one's own way." I am still here. I am not a victim.

We are still here. You and me.

We are following a path, picked and planned, perfectly in line with what we think life is going to be like. We attempt to control what is in our grasp until the unpredictability of it all comes crashing down like a delicate crystal glass dropped on a concrete slab. We are orphans, broken and without hope of life returning to the way it was before this happened.

This.

The accident. The tragedy. The event. The loss.

But what about the emptiness, the suddenness of it? One minute you are texting the one you could never live without, only to find yourself waiting for a reply that never comes. One minute you are walking through that same familiar door only to find something on the other side that leaves you scarred and scared.

This.

Unbeknownst to many, the lasting effect of this lingers like a cobweb woven so tightly, it becomes thicker and even harder to break through as the days and weeks pass. There are no classes in school that teach you how to survive when all you want to do is the opposite. Why do we feel pressure to move forward when going back is the only way to catch our breath and the only way we can make sure the ones we lost are never forgotten?

As I reflect on the last three years of my life, I have no doubt that God has been in complete control. There were times I did not want to acknowledge or believe in God. I was angry. I was sad. I was so confused as to why God would allow all these events to take place in my life. But! Oh, that conjunction makes all the difference in the world—BUT!

But God has a plan for us in our suffering.

When I look at a sunset or smell spring's first rain, I know that I am still here for a reason. I see it now, and I only share it with you because you are still here.

We are still here.

No matter what, God is in control and has a plan. It seems so far-fetched, or as some will say, nonsense. Well, it's not. I have watched the plan play out in my life in real time. How can anyone witness my life over the last three years and think something greater isn't in charge? I'm just a farmgirl, and God is going to use me to help you.

It is crucial to your happiness that you let yourself go to the events in your life. Release your so-called control, of which you really have none. We have no way of knowing what will happen in our lives, as much as we like to think we do. Let God in and put your demands down.

You are never alone. Even in your darkest moments, God is using something within that darkness to help you. Close your eyes and feel that door opening and closing. You may be in charge of opening and closing it, but God provided the door. Open it. Look inside. You will find that you have a reason for living. Living. Learning to live through loss is a skill that may take years to master, but you will come out on the other side understanding your purpose and your path, and there is hope on the other side.

I hope that my life recipe, my journey, and the characters who shaped me will help you get through a time when your world is shattered and everything around you seems meaningless and hopeless.

Just remember, you are still here.

We are still here.

1

Sue

*The best and most beautiful things in the
world cannot be seen or even touched.
They must be felt with the heart.*
—Helen Keller

In 2004, I KNEW it was time to get Momma a cell phone. Daddy was very old-fashioned so all I kept hearing was, "Sue doesn't need a cell phone." However, as much as my parents were helping me with my daughter at that time, I knew Momma not only needed "new technology"—she wanted it. If Daddy had his way, I would be using a quill to write this book. "Something else to break, and something else to fix," as Daddy so frequently said.

I remember telling Momma this would be a great way for us to "talk." So I added a line to our current plan, and on one of our Saturday visits, I took the new phone with me. I don't think any of us realized the incredible freedom she was about to experience. Walking with Momma, I pushed open the front porch screen door, and we ventured into the front yard looking for a better signal and to escape Daddy's anti-technology voice echoing in the house. As I handed her the small Nokia flip phone, she stopped to hold it, cradling it as delicately as she would hold a newborn baby.

As I checked the bars for a signal, we moved a little farther away from the metal roof on our old farm home. We walked just beyond the line of chinaberry trees that separated the front yard from the farm to a more open area free of foliage. Standing along the dusty driveway, me on her left, Momma continued to hold the phone with both hands like it was a grenade that could go off at any moment. We watched the corner of the tiny screen for more bars to fill in. Eventually, Momma became an expert at signal searching. I would see her cell phone left in some of the oddest places—in the branches of a chinaberry tree, on top of the pickup truck, or in the bathroom windowsill that faced north.

I started showing her how texting works. I think she was in shock. She laughed and said, "How about that? Wow!" I explained it was in real time by using my cell phone to return her text as we practiced together. She held the phone in her left hand, gently allowing her right hand to begin typing.

Momma had been an excellent typist, so texting seemed to come naturally for her. It didn't take long, and as with anything she decided to do, she mastered it. Of course, she didn't seem annoyed by the beep-beep-beeps as she scrolled through each number for the right letter. Perhaps this is due to her skilled fingers and the speed of sound. It was so fast that none of us could hear it. She became so good at texting that the repetition of beeps sounded like an advanced telegrapher sending Morse code messages in the peak of warfare.

For most people these days, a cell phone is a necessity for work, pleasure, and, well, everything. In the early 2000s, it was not as crucial to survival as it is now. We keep them near us to feel safe when we are alone or scared. We use them to navigate when driving and to handle anything life may throw our way. They have become our lifeline.

Texting opened a new world for Momma—a normal, hearing one. It was her way of communicating with a world she had never felt a part of in her silence. It became her ears to hear with. For the first time in our lives, we got to talk to Momma without going through Daddy. We shared daily routines, recipes, pictures of food, selfies, and we shared our thoughts on almost everything—precious memories, intimate words. She shared her advice on almost any subject, and she was always there, just a text away.

I think Daddy grew jealous of it in certain ways, but he refused to learn about the latest gadgets. He always left that up to Momma. She was the operator of all things electronic—the VCR, DVD player, resetting the digital clock on the oven and microwave, and even replacing the refrigerator filter.

My momma was deaf from a young age, and what that has taught me about life I never would have learned in any classroom. Just as Momma learned to live without sound, I learned patience, humility, compassion, aggravation, and a deeper love for another human being than I could have ever imagined. I learned to love hard. So hard it hurts. My love comes from a place deep inside, from a place that most people never touch. It's a place that is only found by a few. It's a place that is fragile, guarded, and vulnerable. It's a place that finds you when you're lost and holds you when you fall. It's a place that breaks and shatters when love is lost.

That being said, I was still her daughter, and we had our mother-daughter moments. Whew! I remember being fifteen and mean. I was so angry I couldn't go out to a party that "everyone is going to." I got so upset and yelled "bitch" behind Momma's back, knowing there was no way she heard me. Taking advantage of what I thought was her weakness only proved to show me it was her greatest strength. She turned around, and with her left hand, she slapped me on the cheek. I deserved the punishment I got, and after raising a daughter of my own, she was very gracious in her correction. I deserved much more.

She deserved more.

On November 24, 1944, in an old farmhouse outside of Itasca, Texas, Thelma Fowler Worlow gave birth to a beautiful baby girl, Sue Wynell. It was a cold and windy day, as I heard the story told. The house had big rooms with windows that sifted the wind, creating that whistling sound we associate with winter weather. The Redwine house, as she referred to it from the name of the people who had lived on the farm before, was a special place to Momma. It isn't there anymore; there is only an empty hay field. If everyone who drove by this field knew the miracle that was born there, they would stop to feel the wind against their skin and soak up the spirit of her that I know is still there. This place, the house, the land, and the warmth she felt in her mother's arms were etched in her core memories.

Sue came into this world perfectly healthy, hearing all the sounds. There was no Apgar test at that time, but if there had been, she would have passed with flying colors. A bouncing baby girl hearing birds chirp, screen doors slam, and congregations singing hymns on Sunday mornings.

Her first birthday came and went. Looking back, I realize we never talked much with Momma about her first seventeen months of life. It seemed that her story started at eighteen months, and no one remembered much prior to that. I guess that's how traumatic events affect us. We, unfortunately, begin to use the event as our starting point. That event starts a new calendar, as if the old calendar never existed. Everything begins and ends on that day.

At eighteen months old, my mother became sick with a very high fever that lasted for several days, and as a result, she lost her hearing. The doctor did all he could, but the fever bore its weight in her ears, forever taking away one of her five senses. My grandparents didn't notice immediately. It was an awareness that grew over time when she didn't respond to certain sounds and stopped the normal baby talk my grandparents had heard so often before. There was nothing that could be done. It was hopeless, as life often seems to be. It is in these moments of despair that miracles break through. In my mother's case, it was in the silence that she would later hear what hope sounded like.

Hearing loss was only one event that shaped Sue into the miraculous being who later became my mother. She lived through sexual abuse by molestation. What better prey for a child-molesting monster than an innocent little girl who couldn't speak? I didn't learn of this until just a few years before she died. I had heard hints through the years, but never detailed facts laid out as she did with me on that one summer day. I'll never forget it. She spoke without fear. She spoke with empowerment, possibly from the movement that was growing. She didn't feel alone anymore.

Speaking of uncomfortable things is so important! It's crucial to survival and a necessary ingredient for living. If there is one thing we need to learn above everything else, it is that being silent about uncomfortable things only worsens them, in causes and effects. By sharing, we belong, and by belonging we can share. I saw Momma's ability to speak about what happened to her as another part of her life she was able to conquer. This is where superpowers form and grow.

The loss of her hearing, the abuse, the absence of normalcy during the developmental years—it all shaped her into a unique being who could recognize and understand the intricacies of people. She was always watching, feeling, learning, and modeling the best human behavior that was both elegant and educated.

And when you were around her, you were better for it.

Beauty came effortlessly for Momma. She had thick, wavy hair. Everyone always commented on her natural curls. She kept it above her shoulders, pulled back in a headband or barrette, and sometimes "a little too short" if her hairstylist got distracted. Over the last ten years or so, she let her natural color come through, casting complementary shades of gray, framing her porcelain-like complexion. Her smile was genuine, and when you saw her, you felt comfort and warmth. "She has to run around in the shower to get wet" and "We have to tie a watermelon to her leg to keep her from blowing away," Daddy would jokingly say about Momma's petite frame. Momma had the glamour of Eva Gabor with a mix of Audrey Hepburn and Jacqueline Kennedy, all packaged beautifully together in a quiet, elegant, yet strong woman. She was.

I wish Momma would have had more time to share with all of us. Don't we all wish for more time, more good times? I can close my eyes and see Momma sitting beside me, her hand on my leg, and she is telling me about love, about Jesus, or about how to make a pie crust. I can still close my eyes and see it, feel it, and embrace it. She carried burdens like feathers, never letting anything weigh her down. She was the exception to every rule, the calm to chaos, and she was my momma.

She didn't hear, speak, or communicate "normally" until age ten. My grandparents, Wesley and Thelma, sent her to live with dear family friends so that she could attend Alta Vista Grade School in Waco, Texas, in 1953. The school had resources and teachers who were trained in speech education, speech therapy, and special education. The school my mother left did not have the resources or teachers she needed at that time.

In Waco, my mother was able to be in the least restrictive environment (teacher talk) in a classroom and be with others who were just like her and some "much worse" as she would tell us. She remembers all their disabilities and handicaps, but to her they were just people, her friends, and she loved being with them. She had such fond memories of the years she spent acquiring her first language, and even better memories of the many people she met along the way.

The relationships she formed and held through the years were a testimony to who she was. The teacher who had the most influence and truly gave Momma her voice, Mrs. Pope, came to live near Momma when she got older. What a blessing this was for Momma. She would visit Mrs. Pope in her retirement home almost every day until the end. They had a love for each other that only they understood. It was that deep love. I compare it to the love between Helen Keller and her teacher Anne Sullivan. A love for a life brought forth in a seemingly hopeless world.

Because one of her five senses was gone, that only sharpened the remaining four. She could see beyond a person and behind a headline. She always said, "People don't see themselves." I never knew what she meant by this, but now I do. I look for what is behind a person, behind their eyes, what they're not saying. I look for their story. In all the ways people express their feelings— verbally, physically, silently—people show us who they are. They show us and sometimes they even tell us.

Do we listen?

Most of the time, no.

Momma did, always. The cell phone was such an important part of my life with Momma. She gained independence, and she gained confidence. It gave her access and freedom to express herself from a distance. Even in her texts, love was palpable.

Texting would be the last time I talked to Momma. I smile now at how completely perfect our last text was. "Beautiful" was the last word she would ever send to me, and oh, how it all was.

Beautiful.

Until that day.

Think Points

Exercise in *Learning to Live:*

Write down a good memory from before your loss.

....
....
....
....
....
....
....
....

Now, write down an experience you have had since your loss. It can be as simple as a good cup of coffee, a funny conversation, or a good night's sleep.

....
....
....
....
....
....
....
....

If you can do this once a week, it will help to blend the life you once had with the life you have now.

2

Chocolate-Covered Strawberries

*I write so people can feel what I feel, see what
I see, and love what I have loved.*
—Theo Boyd

IT WAS A MONDAY morning, the start of a very exciting week for me. The school district I worked for agreed to let me be in charge of entertainment for the yearly teacher assembly, and boy, was I going to surprise them with a little celebrity concert. They agreed only because I sat in the superintendent's office one afternoon convincing her that this would be "the concert that all the teachers would love to see, something different and new."

In high school, I performed a routine for a UIL (University Interscholastic League) program that involved a microphone, music, costume, and me. Back then, they had fun little categories in addition to the usual prose, poetry, speech, and ready writing. That year it was a lip-sync competition, and I chose Reba McEntire's "Little Rock." Out of forty high school contestants, I won third place. I am as proud of that win as I am of later being nominated class clown—my claim to fame! As I graduated and began living my life, the Reba routine followed me. I performed it on different occasions, for family reunions, birthday parties, and girlfriend get-togethers. It was always a fun way to get people in the party mood. When the lights and props were good, some people even thought I was her. This was usually the elderly individuals in the audience, but I didn't care. I loved it and still do.

My parents understood my love and fascination for her music and surprised me with my very first concert tickets. They were for REBA! I went to school happier that morning than ever before. It was an experience I will never forget.

My sister and I shared a room. We called our bedroom the blue room because of the shade of pale blue Momma had painted the walls. My sister claims I wouldn't let her "escape the blue room" until she watched me perform every song from Reba's 1986 *Whoever's in New England* album. I remember grabbing my hairbrush, putting on the denim dress with the concho belt I borrowed from Momma's closet, and practicing Reba's unique jaw twist for hours. With Reba, lip-syncing is all skill. I stick by that.

I would walk out of the blue room, lights turned off. My sister would hold the flashlight as my spotlight, Momma would be on their bed, Daddy in his chair, and "Reba" took to the stage, or a shag-carpeted floor in this case. They were all so enduring of what I seemed to never tire of, being Reba, and watching them smile.

Momma never heard the music from the songs, but she would read my lips. Reba's songs seemed to have a feeling in them that I could tell even Momma felt. It may seem silly to some, but in a way, I felt like I was giving Momma music that she could enjoy. She didn't hear it, but she could feel it with me. Momma told us that music sounded like a loud rumble to her. She couldn't hear pitch or melody, only a very unpleasant buzzing sound. The last time she heard anything clearly, the way it was meant to sound, was when she was a baby. Well, and now.

So many things in life we wish would last forever. They don't. The good times, the fun times, and the times that are the most memorable are a combination of the good, the bad, and the ugly. We must not let the bad and ugly times overshadow the good. Some days, it does feel good to fall into the bad and that's okay. Know what it is and know you can and will come out of it.

I felt that all my days would be dark from the moment my nightmare started. I'm not going to lie to you—the good days were few and far between, but it's not the entire day we should look at. We need to think about the times within the day. I may have woken up feeling dark and feeling the hits to my stomach, but in an hour or two, I would get a text or call from a friend and the dark would start to lift a little. So, it's not the entire day; it's the few minutes or hours within that day that matter. Hold on to those. Hold on to them as tightly as you can because those are what will get you through to the next day and the next.

For Momma, living through bad times and knowing "it will all work out" was her mantra. She lived in a world of silence. I took so many things for granted. She didn't. Having never uttered a word until ten years of age and learning how to communicate at that age must have been overpowering and terrifying. For most people, it would be debilitating, but for Momma, it was just another little hurdle to jump.

"Focus on what you have and what you can give to help others," Daddy would always say. "That is where real happiness is." It's in the person who is aware of the world around them and how they fit into it. Knowing why you are you and accepting that, no matter what, is the first step to releasing your power within. And it is in that power where you will find and understand your purpose.

> *You've always had the power my dear, you*
> *just had to learn it for yourself.*
> —Glinda, *The Wizard of Oz*

Monday, July 29, 2019.
The last day Momma was alive.

I didn't want to write that date. I didn't even want to see it written on the paper. It coats me like a bucket of black paint, pouring itself slow and steady. With each hour that passes, the weight of darkness presses down harder until I am completely covered. Like mosquitos that return every spring and sharp grass burrs that sprout each summer, it doesn't go away. When autumn's crisp air blows the leaves from their perch, and when winter's frost comes to blanket them, I am still captive to its darkness.

As I mentioned, it was a Monday. I went to the school that morning to work on the program, met a friend for lunch, and stopped by the grocery store on my way home to buy strawberries and chocolate. I had enough time to get ready for the museum party my husband and I were going to that evening. It was a fundraiser, and each guest was asked to bring a favorite food dish. Chocolate-covered strawberries were my "thing" to bring. We all have our "thing" that we feel is our specialty food item.

Strawberries dipped in milk chocolate and drizzled with thin lines of white chocolate were mine.

I was at home prepping strawberries, selecting a dress to wear that night, and doing laundry. The weather had been milder the week before, but on that day, we reached almost 100 degrees. I had been texting with my sister and Momma all afternoon. We had our group text really going that day. I sent a selfie that morning as I headed out. Momma had responded, letting us know how busy she had been preparing documents for Daddy's neurologist appointment and repotting some plants. She had a busy Monday. From shelling black-eyed peas that she and Daddy had picked to visiting the nursery in town to purchase a new plant or two, she made it a very full day. She always did. If there was work to be done, she was going to do it. And if there wasn't any, she would find some.

Momma and I had a side text going on to finalize our time and meeting place for Daddy's appointment the next day. Cleburne was a pretty good-sized town about forty minutes north of their house and about forty minutes southwest of mine. It was a great halfway place for both of us, and a place my parents visited quite often for certain doctor visits.

Daddy had been diagnosed with White Matter Disease for about a year and had routine visits to keep the progression in check. We learned from doctors and Google that White Matter Disease wears away tissue in the deepest part of the brain. It affects mobility, thinking, and memory and is categorized under the umbrella of dementia and Alzheimer's. It can be genetic and is found most commonly in people with blood pressure issues or who have had strokes. Daddy had three mini-strokes over the past eight years. He, of course, had worked as a farmer all his life, so the chemicals found around a working farm were a contributing factor. We finalized our meeting for the next day. I was going to meet Daddy and Momma at the Johnson County Courthouse in Cleburne at 11:00 a.m.

We planned to eat lunch together, then we were going to Daddy's appointment, and after that, Daddy wanted to take me and Momma to the dress shop that Momma always liked to visit, Cato. He wanted to buy us both something. That was their usual routine, and Momma was so excited that I was going to become a part of it.

It was hard for her to hear and understand everything the doctor would say, especially since this particular doctor had a mustache. So I would start to help Momma with this one part of understanding Daddy's dementia. It was new to all of us.

However, we never made it to that day.

We never met at the courthouse or went to eat lunch.

We never went to the doctor's office, and Daddy didn't get to buy us both a new dress at Cato.

That Monday evening, Momma was killed on the farm. She was accidentally run over by a tractor, and Daddy was sitting in the driver's seat. It was the beginning of our nightmare and the worst thing I have ever experienced.

In the midst of the turmoil and chaos, Daddy kept mentioning appointments that needed to be canceled. My parents were very punctual and never missed an appointment so canceling or not showing up was *not* an option. I remember thinking, *Why does this even matter?* As I stood in the kitchen, looking at the calendar and calling to cancel any scheduled visits, I could see it mattered to Daddy.

With the doorbell and phone competing for our attention, my Type-A personality was put into motion. Each time I heard Daddy say "Goodbye," I would run to grab the phone to take care of business. I remember telling Daddy that he didn't need to stay on the phone so long because we had a lot to get done for Momma's funeral.

I called the doctor's office Tuesday morning from their kitchen and tried to explain what had happened. I don't really remember what I said. I just know that when I finally reached them, after being placed on hold for what seemed like hours, they had already heard the news. When I called Momma's dentist, they, too, had already heard. I was thinking, *How did y'all already hear about this?* but I didn't say anything. I just listened to them say how sorry they were and ask if there was anything they could do. It had only been a little over twelve hours. I got a sense early on of how people in a close-knit community respond when tragedy strikes.

The community showed up. We were being showered with food, prayers, tears, and love. It wasn't the shower I had pictured for their fiftieth wedding anniversary, which was less than six months away. It was a different kind of shower, completely.

Word travels fast with something as horrific as this. This.

Looking back on that day, Momma and I hadn't texted since lunchtime. So at 4:40 p.m., I started up the group text again with a selfie. I don't know why, but I always enjoyed sending Momma crazy, unattractive selfies, and later, an after photo to show that I could look good if I chose to put in the work.

Momma replied to my selfie:

> You look better than me.

I said,

> NO!! Ha ha! I look awful.

Momma always looked beautiful.

At 5:21 p.m., she sent us a selfie showing her sitting up in their bed. She had just taken a shower, washed her hair, and rolled it. She said she was planning to go to bed early after getting everything ready for the next day. The selfie was taken in real time or live, so if you hold your finger on the picture, it moves, and you can see Momma looking at the camera and reaching up to touch her face. These were the last visions I have of her alive. She would have hated knowing that would be the last picture we would see of her, but she would probably say, *Well, that's life.* She seemed to say that for every little thing that life sent our way.

My sister and I both responded with how beautiful she is, without make-up and with her hair in rollers. It was just a regular day of texting and sharing our lives in an intimate, fun group text with Momma.

To keep the text going, I sent a quick shot of the chocolate-covered strawberries chilling in the refrigerator for our evening at the museum.

Momma texted:

> Oh I love it. It's so pretty.

We continued texting for a little while about random things. My sister sent a picture of pork chops in her oven that she was preparing for dinner. We laugh about that now.

We all loved sharing recipes and food pictures. My sister and I learned everything we know about cooking and baking from her. She was the best cook I will ever know. I find myself making her recipes quite often. I remember when I made her old-fashioned Christmas tea cakes, and with the first bite, I immediately started crying. It was her. It was Momma. The taste was the same. I did it. A victory in the kitchen! I successfully made the cookies, but why did I feel so defeated? They didn't bring her back in physical form, but in a way, they did by memory, just for a minute.

At 5:25 p.m., I sent a picture of the brightly colored jacket, covered in sequins, that the backup singers were going to wear in the Reba concert.

My sister said:

Yay!

and Momma texted back:

Wow, it's beautiful.

We didn't know it at the time, but "beautiful" was the last word Momma would text to my sister and me in the group text. How fitting. How ironic. How perfect. Her last word typed to us was what she was.

—Beautiful—

I quickly took my shower and decided I would use this evening as a test run on the Reba make-up and trying on the wig. The blush and mascara went on a little heavier than I normally wear, and I put liner around the curves of my lips to help them stand out a little more. I was preparing for the ultimate selfie for the group chat.

At 6:36 p.m., I sent what I thought was a good Reba-like picture and waited for a reply. I figured my sister was busy getting dinner on the table for her family. I thought

Momma must have gotten busy with her paperwork for Daddy. I never got a reply. I continued to get dressed, touching the screen on my phone occasionally to see if there were any replies. I knew she would say something like *You look just like Reba!* or *Looks so good!* Momma was always a cheerleader for us. I knew what she was going to say, but I couldn't wait to see it. She always, *always* gave us positive words and complimented us. I didn't realize how much I relied on her affirmations. I continued to check my phone while brushing my teeth. Nothing . . .

At about 6:55 p.m., my husband came in to get dressed for our night. He was running behind so we only spoke briefly. Right before I put on my dress, I went into the kitchen to take the chocolate-covered strawberries out of the refrigerator. I laid the strawberries on the counter to begin transferring them over to the crystal dish I would take to the party. Our home phone rang. We had a land-line phone, but the only calls we ever received on that phone were from Daddy or telemarketers.

I answered. There was a man on the other line, but it wasn't Daddy.

"Is this Mr. and Mrs. Boyd's daughter?"

I said, "Yes."

"There has been an accident, and you need to come to the farm and be with your father as quickly as possible."

"Who are you?" To this day, I do not remember who he was or what department he was with. It was just a voice I never wanted to hear. It was the voice that still haunts me if I let it.

My attention was hyperfocused on what he was saying, all the while trying to make sense of it and coming up with more questions:

Why did someone else have access to their phone?

How did they get my phone number?

Who are they?

Why didn't Momma text me?

Do I need to come now?

Can I come later?

What is going on?

I started shaking and running back and forth from my bedroom to the kitchen.

The voice on the other end of the line continued to repeat, "You need to come to the farm as quickly as possible."

He added, "You need to come be with your dad. There has been an accident. He is in the ambulance."

As I could understand it, my dad was hurt because he was in an ambulance. It had never crossed my mind that Momma might be the one hurt. Not yet.

"Where are you taking him?" I asked.

He replied, "No, we aren't taking him anywhere."

"What hospital are you taking him to, and can I meet y'all there?"

He got frustrated as he exhaled. He was stressed for sure. I remember the quiver in the voice.

Beginning to get angry, I insisted, "Where are you taking him? What hospital?"

He said, "We aren't taking him to the hospital. You don't understand. We just need you to get to the farm, please. How long will it take for you to get here?"

I said, "One hour," and then I continued to pepper him with questions.

"Where is my mom? Please just tell me what is going on."

He replied, "Ma'am, can you just get here?"

"I'm on my way."

I knew our conversation was just going in circles. I knew I needed to get in the car and get there. I knew something was not right.

I ran into the bedroom and told my husband. We both agreed it sounded crazy, and I started to make up scenarios that maybe it was a hostage situation and people were at my parents' home wanting money. Many years before, there had been an elderly couple just a few miles from our farm who were murdered one night in their home because they couldn't agree with some men on a price for their guns in a garage sale. The men showed up later that evening and shot them both dead. I thought this could be something like that.

As we ran out of the house to get in my SUV, I asked my husband to call my sister on the speakerphone. He was telling her about the phone call. I got our dog, Manly, and loaded him in the back seat. Knowing how I am, my sister's first words to me were, "Okay, calm down." She knows me well. I said, "I am calm!" Obviously, I was not.

We left. I was driving. Fast.

I never realized it at the time, but that would be the last time I drove away from my home with a mother. I know that seems weird, but I remember things based on when I had something or when I didn't. Even on a vacation, I will say, "Last year at this time, we were . . ." I have always done that. It's like a time association, a dividing line between past and present.

I drove about 85–95 mph, and I remember thinking, *I have to get there and get this all straightened out. Momma is probably confused and doesn't know what to do. Maybe she can't text because they have her phone or she . . .*

This is when it occurred to me—in this moment.

OH, NO! What if Momma is hurt? When it circled back in my thoughts, I yelled it out loud. "What if it's Momma?!"

My husband called one of my dear friends, Dina, who knew my parents well, and he asked her if she had ever heard of anything like this, a man calling but not telling us anything over the phone. She was not on speaker, so I didn't hear everything she said, but I did hear my husband say, "Yes, I think so too." I said, "Think what? What?" He handed me the phone. I said, "Dina, what do you think?" I could tell she didn't want to say. She just said, "Call me when you get there. Drive safe, and I love you."

While I was driving with a laser focus on the road, it came to me that we should call one of my parents' neighbors. The Snow family lived right down the road from the farm, about a mile. *Maybe they knew what was going on?*

Pat Snow was my mom's best friend, and her family was family to us. Pat's mother and my grandmother had been best friends in the community, Bethel. That is the name of the little piece of country where our farm is.

We asked Pat if she could have Shari, her daughter, go by Momma and Daddy's house. We were on our way, but it was still going to be about forty-five minutes. Pat called her daughter, and it just so happened that she was on her way home from work and said she would be happy to drop by and check things out. She promised to call when she got there.

My heart was racing, my mind was blowing up with thoughts.

I texted Momma, and I wasn't getting a response. It was telling. Momma always responded when it was something about Daddy or anything that might be wrong. My imagination was running as fast as I was driving.

Maybe she had broken her arm or leg.

Maybe Daddy had another stroke, and she was in the ambulance with him.

Maybe Momma fell from a tree or got caught in a fence or a cow kicked her.

Maybe she fell off the lawnmower or had a heart attack. She did have a heart arrhythmia and took a mild heart medication. All those thoughts swirled, stirred, and simmered in my mind as I drove back home.

We finally got to the turn where the pavement became gravel. For some reason, I slowed down, almost to a stop, when my wheels hit the dirt. I could feel every piece of white, chalky gravel under my tires. *Why was I going so slow? Right now, everything is the same. Right now, life hasn't changed. Right now, everything is okay.* Even though

I didn't want to, I continued to move forward. Somehow, I knew it was Momma. I had known it from the moment we had gotten in the car, but my mind was protecting me from what my heart felt. I just knew.

When we turned from the gravel road to their private driveway, we still had a little way to go. Their driveway was beautiful and scenic with a small pond on the right-hand side, and usually several cows standing along the water's edge.

We built them a new home in 2013. It was the brick home that Momma had always dreamed of, sitting on top of a small hill that looks out as far as the eye can see. A valley sits below, just beyond the red rock hill with fields of mesquite trees and wild thistle surrounding the view. This land has been in my family for over a century. She loved her new home. It was located right across the gravel road from the old farmhouse I grew up in. After one month in the new home, Momma told me, "If I died today, I would be so happy because I had this house." I said, "Momma, you have only been moved in for one month. Don't die yet." We laughed together.

As I drove closer to the house, I saw lights flashing, people, cars, trucks, emergency vehicles, and an ambulance. The sun was sitting on the edge of the tank berm, and it wouldn't be long until it faded away. All the light was about to leave.

I suddenly remembered that I had left the chocolate-covered strawberries out on my kitchen counter. I should have brought them with me for Momma and Daddy to eat or put them back in the refrigerator so they wouldn't melt.

Isn't it funny how amid frightening and life-changing events, our mind jumps back to our everyday routine? We default to autopilot because the realization that we can control our life is gone and too hard to admit or acknowledge.

We still think of things like putting something back in the refrigerator. Our mind shifts from its normal position back and forth and sideways. We are a compass with a broken needle, rapidly moving in all directions with no set point to ground us.

In that moment, it felt good to think of the chocolate-covered strawberries.

I put the car in park, turned off the engine, and got the leash for Manly out of the small compartment inside my driver's side door. I opened the back door, attached the leash, and he jumped out. As I approached the walkway, everyone was just staring at me. There were at least ten emergency personnel walking around, but only one man from the Hill County Sheriff's Department approached me, and then I saw Shari. I realized she never called. I wasn't ready to hear anything. I told everyone I had to go to the bathroom. I remember holding Manly's leash and telling anyone who came close to me that "I'll be right back." In other words, give me a minute.

When I went to the front door, I walked inside with Manly, and it was quiet and still. While I was in the bathroom, I looked and saw the beautiful shower curtain that I had just bought for Momma two weeks before. It had crystal hooks, and it was white and silver. Momma loved it and couldn't wait to put it up. I helped her get it all hooked, and we admired it together.

As I washed my hands, Manly was just sitting on the floor of the bathroom looking up at me. I started calling out Momma's name. "Momma, Momma. Where are you? Are you lost?"

As I walked around the house, I continued yelling "Momma. Where are you?" My concern was growing. She couldn't hear, so I'm sure people just didn't understand that. I was on a mission to locate my Momma when I remembered I needed to go back outside. I noticed the documents were all laid out on the kitchen island for Daddy's doctor appointment the next day. I briefly looked around the kitchen, calling out her name a few more times. I knew I needed to do the responsible thing and go hear what the deputy had to say. I went to the front door, opened it, and stepped back out to the chaos of lights and grim faces.

Unknowingly, it would be the first time I walked out of Momma's house without her. I heard the deputy tell Shari something, and I heard Shari say, "Oh, me?" I knew she was about to tell me something I never wanted to hear but had to.

As she approached, I could hear Daddy screaming in the ambulance that was parked in their gravel driveway. I wondered what was going on, and I got angry. I couldn't make out Daddy's words, they were too muffled or jumbled. I said, "Can someone please just tell me what the hell is going on?" Shari came up to me, tears rolling down her face, and she said, "Sue is gone." I said, "What do you mean she's gone?" Shari repeated, "Sue is gone. She died." I knew it was so terribly hard for her. I saw the tears streaming down her face, one by one. I can still see them fall.

"I don't understand. I don't understand." I kept saying. That's when the deputy came up and said, "Your dad wasn't sure, but he said his foot slipped off the clutch, and the tractor ran over your mother."

I don't remember exactly what happened next. The wave of sadness, the confusion—the unexpected tragedy . . . it rushed over me. My fog had just started. I don't know if I sat down, fell down, laid down, or what I did—I just know I was suddenly on the ground right by Momma's pampas grass. She loved that plant so much. She had wanted one for so long and finally got it just a few years before, and it was beautiful. So full and healthy. Momma had a green thumb, that was for sure. That pampas grass and me being on the ground at that moment was the last thing I remember after I heard the worst news I had ever heard in my life.

I wish I could have seen her when she first heard an angel's voice. It is supposed to be a sound like we have never heard before, but for Momma so much more. No more buzzing or unpleasant ringing in her ears—just pure, pitch-perfect sound coming from trumpets, angels singing, and the swish of butterfly wings in the air.

Staring at the pampas grass in a daze, it could have been a few minutes later or more than a few—I really don't know. One of the responders came up and asked if we could go to be with Daddy in the ambulance. I looked at my husband and said, "Can you go, please?" He did. Something told me at that point that I couldn't. I just couldn't.

Shari asked one of the responders if she could call her mom. They wouldn't let her tell anyone until I had been told. She called her, my momma's best friend. Still, I couldn't bear to be near Shari while she called to deliver the news a second time. Pat must have been worried since she had not heard from any of us for quite a while. Slowly, I got to my feet. In my bewildered haze, I walked toward the ambulance, reached for the door, and took the steps up to go inside.

Daddy was lying on the stretcher. I bent over to hug him as he wailed, "I killed your mother. I killed her. I am so sorry. Oh, God, what have I done? I'm sorry I killed your mother. God damn, God damn, God damn!" The words came fast, hard, and heavy. They were loaded with pain, shock, and gut-wrenching agony. The darkest, deepest, most lamenting words, moans, and screams. Daddy hugged me hard. I remember my husband telling Daddy to stop saying he killed her—it was an accident. It was an accident.

The emergency responders said the accident happened at approximately 6:00 p.m. Sometime right around 5:30 p.m., Daddy had decided to go check his tractor's battery. I had heard Daddy say for years, "If you leave a tractor too long without cranking it, it won't start."

Daddy continued to cuss and yell out, "I'm sorry, I didn't mean it. Oh, God, what have I done?" I knew what he was saying—he felt 100 percent responsible, but it wasn't his fault. This was an accident.

A tragic accident, the worst kind, the kind when you lose someone you love so deeply.

Oh, how I wish that damn tractor would never have started.

Think Points

☑ Is there a text message or voice mail from your loved one that you keep close to your heart?

....

....

....

....

....

....

....

....

....

☑ What is the last word you heard or saw?

....

....

....

....

....

....

....

....

....

....

....

....

....

....

Sue Boyd

November 24, 1944 ~ July 29, 2019

Sue Boyd passed away at her home in Whitney on Monday, July 29, 2019, at the age of 74. Funeral services will be held at 11:00 a.m. Saturday, August 3, 2019, at Marshall & Marshall Funeral Directors Chapel in Hillsboro with Pastor David Gant and Rev. Roy Frink officiating. Burial will follow at Peoria Cemetery. Visitation will be held from 6:00–8:00 p.m. Friday, August 2, at the funeral home.

Sue was born to Isaac Wesley and Thelma (Fowler) Worlow, November 24, 1944, in Itasca, Texas. When she was only 18 months old, a high fever took her hearing leaving her alone in a world of silence. At the age of ten and with the support of her loving parents, Sue moved to Waco where she attended a specialized school that taught her to communicate and allowed her to continue her seemingly fearless pursuit overcoming life's obstacles.

Sue graduated from Itasca High School in 1964, attended Hill Junior College, and worked as a nanny in San Francisco. In 1968, she returned to Hillsboro and worked at First National Bank in Dallas.

On January 10, 1970, Sue was united in marriage to the love of her life, Joe Bob Boyd, and in a small country home on a hillside, she was a preacher's wife, farmhand, a beloved mother, a dear grandmother, and a 32-year member of Bethel Bible Church where she lived her life to the fullest with grace, beauty, and timeless elegance. This coming January, Sue and Joe would have celebrated their 50-year love story, which was filled with laughter, peanuts, and Jesus.

Preceding her in death were her parents and two sisters, Francis Aline Fowler and Patsy Smith. Survivors include her loving husband of 49 years, Joe Bob Boyd; two daughters, Thelizabeth Boyd and husband, and Hannah Jo Boyd and husband; and three grandchildren, Reagen Thomas, Jonah Locke, and Henry Hehmann.

"Strength and honour are her clothing; and she shall rejoice in time to come." Proverbs 31:25

Sue Worlow Boyd, 1969

3

What the Fuck?

*Say the words that hold the weight of your
pain, no matter what the words are.*
—Loretta Gale Frazier

I HAVE FILLED THIS BOOK with wise words from the two most influential women in my life—Momma and my counselor, Gale. They are both gone now. Gale died suddenly six months after my mother's death and just two weeks after I completed my complicated grief counseling with her. I had a relapse and lost ground in my recovery after Gale died. But it's not how much ground we lose; it's how we get up from the ground and keep walking forward.

Loretta Gale Frazier was my counselor, therapist, confidant, and friend for almost nineteen years. She counseled me through a marriage that ended in divorce, raising a teenage daughter, and a blended family. Going above and beyond, she was there for weekly texts and talks most of my adult life. If I had been a contestant on the game show *Who Wants to Be a Millionaire?*, Gale would have been my lifeline. She was consistently there for me and always had a few simple pearls of wisdom to share that could get me "off the roof" and back into my living room. It's important to have someone who can give you a truthful, educated, professional, yet compassionate answer to life's never-ending questions. The never-ending questions! It seems that just when I thought I had life figured out, another problem, catastrophe, concern, or question would come to mind, and I found myself right back in my usual spot talking to Gale.

Since Gale and I shared more than just a typical counselor/patient relationship, I had access that most of her other clients did not. Mine was almost unlimited. I say almost because there were a few times that I reached out but knew she was probably not going to get back with me until the next day or so. In most situations, this was fine because it was only a concern or question. I could wait a few days to hear how to manage a teenager, a marital issue, or a minor life struggle. The night of July 29, 2019, as my shaking fingers typed out a text, I prayed this wasn't one of those times I would have to wait. It was about 10:30 p.m., and I walked outside for just a minute to breathe.

I texted Gale.

> I know it's late, but my mom was killed in a farming accident today, and my dad is saying horrible words and cursing God. He accidentally ran over her with the tractor, and she is dead. I just don't know what to do.

Within minutes, Gale texted me back.

> Oh no, I am so sorry. Let your dad say the words he wants to say, no matter what they are. Those words carry the weight of what he is feeling. Be kind to yourself. I'll call you tomorrow.

I began to breathe again. I needed to hear some direction, some instruction, and not a Bible verse, a moan, a scream, or the sound of sobbing.

Over the next few days, weeks, and months, I had several one-on-one sessions with Gale. I was able to take Daddy three different times to her office, about an hour north of Whitney. Daddy's best friend lived in the same town so it made for a full day of visiting with friends and then going to counseling. Daddy grew to love Gale. She was a tremendous help and resource for us during this difficult, most unbearable time.

The first appointment I had in her office after the accident is one I will never forget. I sat down on the couch, facing her at an angle across the room. She had her notepad and pen in hand. I can only imagine what my file looked like with almost two decades of notes.

Gale had only moved once since we had been visiting each other. The first time I went to see her, the office was located right beside the main train tracks that run through Duncanville, Texas. Almost near the center of downtown, she had a comfortable space in an office building that had numerous other businesses inside. We would laugh because it seemed that my visits would always be at the same time as the 4:00 or 5:00 train was coming through. We would talk a little louder, and my gift from Momma of reading lips kicked in.

Gale's new office was just down the road from the first, and she was on the second floor. You could take an elevator or use the stairs, whichever you felt like. I usually took the stairs, trying to get my steps in, but I noticed that when I got into her office, I was winded and could barely talk. So I started using the elevator, usually putting on some lip gloss during the ride up.

My visits with Gale were usually "What's going on?" "How are you?" "How's work?" "Catch me up on things."

This visit was different. She came in the room, sat in her chair across from me, dropped her arms and pen heavily down on her notepad, looked right at me, took in a deep breath, and on the exhale said, "What the fuck?!" Having never heard a curse word come from her lips, we both just looked at each other for a second and busted out laughing. I was laughing while tears dropped and rolled down my cheeks.

Over the years, Gale had gotten to know my family from my stories, trials, struggles, and just our chats about life situations. Gale knew the regard with which I held my mother. "I feel like I know your mom. I can't imagine what this feels like for you."

I did my normal spill-all-my-guts talking and she took a few notes. We cried, we laughed, she guided me, and she gave my feelings a name.

Gale said, "You are in complicated grief." I said, "What? Oh my gosh—there's a name for this? That makes sense. Yes, thank God there is a name for it. Maybe I'm not going completely crazy." She replied, "No, you are not. What you are experiencing is heavy, weighted, and you have to treat it delicately. You need to be kind to yourself. Be very gentle with yourself." I spelled it aloud as I typed it in my phone, "C-o-m-p-l-i-c-a-t-e-d Grief." I wanted to make sure I was getting the term exactly right. "It can be complex or complicated, but that is what you are experiencing. You need to keep coming to see me, and I would like to finally meet your dad."

In other words, Gale knew we needed some intense counseling. I kept thinking, *Wow! This must be bad. I am in complicated grief, and she wants to see Daddy.*

Since my journey through complicated grief started at the beginning of August, school was about to start, and I knew my school needed to know what was going to happen with my classes. I knew I could not teach. Not yet. I contacted a dear teacher friend, Amberly, the week of the funeral while I was in planning mode and thinking strategically. I asked her to please get in touch with whomever to help me with family leave paperwork. Being able to delegate responsibilities had never been my strong suit, but I'm a quick learner.

I remember getting all the papers from the school, working through them the best I could, and taking them to Gale for the professional diagnosis and signature required. She had to complete and sign several pages. When I left her office, I opened the envelope and peeked through the papers like a spy uncovering top-secret information. I saw the page that discussed my condition. Gale had written:

> *Complex Grief symptoms after the tragic loss of her mother. In addition, patient is currently caring for her father while being treated for a condition known as Complicated Grief.*

I was able to take six weeks off, with pay, and get life figured out. The new normal people mentioned was beginning, whether I liked it or not. I hated that term "new normal," and I still do. Gale didn't use it, so neither would I. In my opinion, normal had died on July 29, 2019.

I did not have a term for what my future would look like, but I didn't want a new normal—I wanted my old normal back. I still had Daddy, my daughter, and my husband, or so I thought. They were all still in my picture, along with the memory of Momma. She was the background that covered the entire canvas, and we were all small translucent figures lying on top. Without her, the painting would be empty, blank, and void of any color.

It was late in August 2019 when I got Daddy's first appointment with Gale. It was the first of three in-person visits he would have. I didn't know how he was going to be in this appointment. I sat in with them for a while. That was the plan. Gale and I had spoken previously about how the session would look. She thought it would be best if we stayed together for the first visit or the first thirty minutes. Then she said I could step out to visit the bathroom and let her talk with Daddy alone.

The first visit was good. It went better than any of us expected. Daddy seemed so relieved to have someone to talk to about his pain. It dawned on me in that first visit, Daddy had always been the one to hear everyone else's pain all through the years, much like Gale. They shared an immediate bond that neither of them acknowledged, but I saw it. Daddy had counseled people for over thirty-three years, ministering to the community through our little country church—Bethel Bible Church. Gale had been counseling people for about the same amount of time. She was a year younger than Daddy, the same age as Momma.

During the next visit, I excused myself a little earlier in the session. I thought it would be good for Daddy to have some alone time to discuss whatever he wanted. I went to the bathroom because I always have to do that, and when I returned to the waiting area, I didn't sit. Instead, I went up to the door that separated Gale and Daddy from me. I sat down along the wall and leaned over to the door, cupped my right hand over my ear, and listened, just like a child eavesdropping on her parents' private conversation. I was curious about the accident. I still didn't have all the answers that I wanted.

Just two days after the accident, my sister and I had made a break for it, leaving some visitors and Daddy back at the house. We walked across the road to the old farmhouse where the tractor was. We were walking fast, light on our feet, like intruders trying to escape the scene before anyone called the police. We both had the same intense desire to know exactly how this happened and to quench a small amount of our thirst for answers.

We made our way through the barbed wire gate that we had opened and shut for years, going into the pasture that circled our old home. The part of the gate you held to open was a collection of Daddy's old baling wire hooks and latches, his repeated attempts to keep the gate secure through the years.

We walked with purpose, waving with a guilty feeling to cars passing by. "We're okay; just taking a little walk." Everyone in the community seemed focused on our family. It was comforting and appreciated, but when out doing investigative work, it was hampering our mission. We didn't want to tell anyone that we were going to the scene of the accident to see exactly how our Daddy ran over Momma.

What would they think?

Would they try to stop us?

Would they want to go with us?

We wanted to do it alone. Quietly. We wanted to see or smell or understand something for ourself. We had to know.

My sister walked around the south side of the tractor heading to the front, while I stood looking at the steps facing north that led up to the seat. I looked down and I saw the sand. There was a break in the normal lay of the ground. There was dead grass, weeds, dirt, and rock everywhere, but in this one spot, measuring about three feet long and two feet wide, there was a perfectly raked piece of ground. Someone had smoothed the ground to cover any evidence of Momma and her tragic death. Whoever it was, they didn't want us to see anything bad. Instead, we had to use our imagination for that.

We stood and looked, no words said. I knew we should be heading back, and my sister felt the urgency as well. We stopped for a second to check our phones. No one had contacted us yet. We hesitated to go back, as we had only spent minutes at the tractor, and returning without even a bit of closure would feel like a failed mission.

Our old basketball goal, just ten feet away from where we were standing, was whispering to me. I could still hear the laughter and the sound of the ball hitting the backboard as I stood there in the same air that Momma had breathed in her last breath. I could picture her standing there with the ball, and all of us playing "Around the World." Momma yelling out when she made a basket and Daddy being frustrated because he didn't.

As we continued to search for answers, I bent down, squatting, putting my weight on my heels, also to hide from any more passersby. Then something caught my eye. I looked up at the tire right in front of me. I could see a reflection of something contrasting with the darkness of the tread. It was waving. I slowly started to stand and look closer, my right hand reaching out for it. I touched the shiny, almost microscopic object with my index finger. I leaned forward to get a closer look, my nose almost touching the tire, and I felt it, stopping its reflection.

"It's Momma's hair! Hannah! Hannah!"

Proof of her very existence waving as if to say *Yes, it's me. I'm here.* A few strands of Momma's gray, naturally wavy hair were wedged in a tiny crack of the tread, and there was no mistaking it. It was her. Even in the grossest and most horrific moment, she was still there and beautiful. Her hair was still beautiful.

My constant quest for answers to the nightmare would go on for years, but little by little, I would find out enough to get me through each passing day.

Back at Gale's office, I could hear Momma telling me that it was okay to listen, to find out the truth of what happened. Raw and unfiltered, I heard it all. Daddy needed to tell it, and whether he knew this or not, I needed to hear it.

As Gale spoke softly, Daddy didn't. I was familiar with both of their voices.

"Do you want to talk about what happened?" Gale prompted.

"Yes, yes, I do," Daddy replied. "I was worried that if I didn't start those tractors the batteries would die. Once . . ." Daddy went into the *Farmer's Almanac* version of explaining tractors, batteries, and exactly how they all work or don't. I leaned in closer, hugging the door to make a suction cup of my ear against the tunnel I made with the outer edge of my hand.

"Well, it had been a while, and I thought I would check out our old International Harvester 1468. I call it our "Big Red" tractor. Sue didn't have to go. I told her I could do it. She came with me and helped me a little to get up in the tractor seat. She held the battery while I cranked it, and it did—it cranked! Whew! We were both so happy it started. I couldn't believe it started. There was a man interested in buying it just a few days before, and when we were over there, it wouldn't crank. So we charged the battery and sure enough, it worked," Daddy continued explaining. I sat motionless on the floor, still cupping my ear so I didn't miss a word. I couldn't believe I was finally going to get answers to the questions my mind kept asking.

"Sue climbed back down. She turned around. Why did she turn around?" Daddy began to sob. He moaned in the same hums and sounds I heard the night this happened.

"She turned around and handed me the battery box and all the cables that came out of the box and wires. She was handing them up to me. When I reached over to get them, I guess my left foot slipped off the clutch."

Silence. Daddy stopped making any noise. *Did they hear me outside the door?* I was doing my best not to make a sound. I was putting a mouse to shame.

"She turned around. I reached down, and my foot slipped. I thought the tractor was in neutral, but it wasn't, it wasn't! It must've slipped into gear from the jostling of being on. It was in High-1. That's the fastest gear, and you can't stop it, boy. It happened so fast. It was so fast."

Gale continued to listen, with occasional deep breaths. Daddy continued to tell it all.

"It all happened so fast. I knew. I just knew I had killed her. I got down, but I knew. I went over to her." Daddy was sobbing and telling Gale exactly what happened. I knew he needed to tell someone.

"I'm so glad my girls didn't see what I saw. I saw her there, dead. There was no doubt she was dead. I laid my head down on her chest. I just laid there with her, and Barney, our dog, came over sniffing and laid there with us. He loved Sue. He knew something was wrong. I laid there with her, and I even wanted to go with her. I thought about it. I told the sheriff I was going to."

Gale interrupted, "Going to what, Joe Bob?"

"I thought about taking my life, so I could be with Sue. But I didn't want Thelizabeth and Hannah to always wonder what happened to their mother and daddy."

There was silence. I pictured Gale sitting, her right arm bent, holding her pen to her lips, and Daddy sitting with his eyes closed, recalling it all through the steady stream of tears rolling down his face. Then Daddy continued, and I moved in closer to the door.

"A little while went by, and I got up and knew I needed to call the sheriff's office. I drove back on our 4-wheeler and got to our phone. I got the phonebook to look for their number, but while I was fumbling through the pages, I saw that page with 911. I had never called that before, but I called it. I figured this was a time that I should call that number."

I knew Daddy had been frustrated about having to leave Momma and call for help. He kept telling us how he wanted to go be with Momma and how he eventually hung up on the 911 operator.

"The woman answering wouldn't quit asking me questions. I told her I ran over my wife on the tractor. She's dead. I finally had to tell her I was going to go be with my wife. I gave her the address and then told her I was going to hang up. By the time we hung up, the ambulance was already outside. She kept me on the phone for a long time."

"When I went outside, they were there. They followed me back over to the farm across the road. Sue was there, but they had put a blanket over her. I didn't want to leave her. I wanted to stay there. They put me in the ambulance, and I never even knew they drove us back over to our front yard at our new house. It was awful."

Gale proceeded to explain to Daddy that losing a spouse is the worst kind of loss. "The loss of a spouse is one of the hardest losses that there is." Daddy found comfort in her words; he found validation for his grief. He found a confidant, much as I had with Gale over the years.

It was through this validation that Daddy saw some glimmer of hope. I found out from Gale, in our next counseling session alone, that I needed to let go of the possibility of happiness ever returning to him. "You can be there for him, love him, and make sure he is safe, but don't think you can bring happiness back to his life."

In these words, reality hit me hard. My daddy couldn't be happy again? There would be times we would laugh in the next few months and years, but the laughs were never the same. Gale had been right about that.

I decided I had better get up from my seat on the hallway floor and act like I hadn't heard anything. I brushed myself off, slapped my face a little to bring me back to the present, and knocked lightly on the door. Neither Gale nor Daddy ever shared more than "losing a spouse is one of the most difficult losses" and "be kind to yourself." I got much more out of their session than they ever realized—I got answers about what exactly happened and what Momma's last few moments on earth were like.

Listening to Daddy recount the accident was good for him and for me. I was so thankful for Gale. Without her,

Daddy wouldn't have been able to get this out. For the next four months, Gale would call Daddy weekly. It was so helpful for him. "I love Gale. She is so good to talk to," Daddy would say.

I remember when I had to tell him Gale passed away. I didn't know how I was going to do it, but I did. We both cried on the phone with each other.

On February 7, 2020, I was teaching class. It was the last period on a Friday, students were silently reading, and I glanced at my phone to see the text that had just come through.

> Did you know that Gale Frazier died this morning?

These words came through before I even touched the screen. I clicked to verify what I was reading. I began to breathe heavily, and I walked out of my classroom with the intention to walk right out the school doors. I frantically tried to find an aide in the hallway to cover my class. I left the door to the room open and started to just bawl my eyes out. The teacher across the hall and the one next door to my room heard me and came running. "What's wrong, Theo?"

They all knew who Gale was. I talked about her all the time and shared her wisdom. They also knew she was playing a crucial role in my healing journey. They were speechless. I'm sure they thought, *Oh geez, what is Theo going to do now? She may break.*

I just sat in the hallway and cried. They patted my back, hugged me, and said they were so sorry. A student came from my room. "I read the last part of our book to the class. We are all worried about you. It'll be okay. We love you." Sometimes, just having one of your students step up in that adult role can be all the consoling a person needs.

The final bell for the day was about to ring so I grabbed my things and left school early. The teachers covered my class for those last few minutes.

Those last few minutes . . . *what happened to Gale?*

As I recall our last session, when I got up to leave, she asked if I wanted a drink from her office fridge. "Sure, that actually sounds good." She returned with the cold bottle of green tea, and without hesitation, I said, "I love you." She said, "I love you, too, and I always have." I knew she looked frail the last time I saw her, but I never dreamed this could happen. Maybe she did.

Gifts from Gale. They are too numerous to fit in this book. I will share as much from Gale as I can, but look for my next book. If I am to include everything this woman helped me with, there will be another book for sure.

Think Points

☑ Be kind to yourself.

☑ Don't expect too much from yourself. If you don't feel like getting out of bed, don't. It's okay to lie in bed. Know that soon you will be able to get up. Just not today.

☑ Don't put pressure on yourself to be anything you "think" you need to be. Be in the moment and listen to your body.

☑ Talk to someone. It is so crucial to your mental well-being that you seek professional advice during your grief. I can't tell you how much this helped and still helps me. Family and friends mean well, but it is best to turn to someone who is trained in grief counseling.

☑ Look for positive affirmations in your life. If there is a friend who texts to check on you or an employer who is being sensitive to your grief, allowing you additional time off, embrace it. It is in those little gestures that you are receiving love, so do just that—receive it!

....

....

....

....

....

Bittersweet: Momma loved how she looked in this photo, 2010. Little did we know that she was standing in front of the tractor that would later end her life so tragically.

4

What Is Grief Anyway?

*The days following a tragic loss are blurred, but
the months and years will become crystal clear.*
—Theo Boyd

A GONY, HEARTBREAK, MISERY, PAIN, worry, head-aches, vomiting, diarrhea. Those last two most won't talk about or admit, but they are very real. They come naturally, without warning, when you are suffering from tragic loss.

How is it possible that a one-syllable, five-letter word can hold such a multitude of emotions and symptoms that cripple every part of our body? I mean, completely shut down from the inside out? My acronym for grief looks like this:

G – Gutting
R – Raw
I – Indescribable
E – Everlasting
F – Fear (I wanted to write "fuck" right here.)

Grief is the table that holds all these feelings. Those of you in these dark days have taken a seat like an unwel-come guest, required to stay, not wanted, and desperately wishing you could walk away. We don't want anything on this table. We don't want to be here as much as it doesn't want us. It's like a child looking at a plate of raw vegeta-bles. Yuck!

We are taught to love and belong to people, but then all of a sudden, when the person you loved and belonged to the most is gone, there is no one to tell you what you are supposed to do. Gale was trying to help. Now she is gone too. What the fuck is right!

Albert Schweitzer said, "In everyone's life, at some time, our inner fire goes out. It is then burst into flame by an encounter with another human being." I'm just a farmgirl from a small town in Texas. I am sharing what I have learned living with grief.

Each of us grieves each loss we
experience in a unique way.
—Dr. Katherine Shear

Complicated grief disorder, or CGD, is now known as prolonged grief disorder, or PGD. Many of the resources that focus on the symptoms of this particular grief and the behavior of the grieving individual say that an estimated 10 to 15 percent of those grieving will experience PGD. That is out of approximately 70 percent who are grieving.

You may wonder what the difference is between grief and complicated grief. In my explanation of what "normal" grief or loss is, I like to think of this scenario:

A loved one dies, you go to the funeral, and you return to work the next day. You are sad, but after the funeral you decide to go to a Mexican restaurant, and have a margarita.

When explaining complicated grief, the scenario looks more like this:

A loved one dies, and you go to the funeral. You do not return to work. The thought of going out appalls you. You completely shut down.

Complicated grief is not only the way a person reacts to the loss, but it can be caused by how they lost that person. Sudden, tragic, unexpected. It sucks! That's one way to put it. In other words, complications get in the way of adapting to the loss. Work or going out sounds like something you did in a previous life and will never do again.

Until I knew my grief had a name, I thought I was losing my sanity minute by minute. People would talk or say something to me, and I would stare into space. The thought of having to keep my mind focused on anything for more than two seconds became frustrating. I lost my equilibrium. My body was off. I was off.

I was running on autopilot with an empty fuel tank. My normal brain function was hampered by shock and disbelief, and the physical pain I was in quickly seeped into my mental state as well. Eating, sleeping, and any form of a routine in my life had disappeared.

A few days after Momma's accident, I decided to get on our Ranger ATV (all-terrain vehicle) that we kept on the farm. I wanted to ride over to check on a few things. I wasn't sure what exactly, but I wanted and needed to get out for a bit. There were plenty of people still coming in and out of the house to keep Daddy company, so I knew he would be okay.

As I drove through the pasture where all of Daddy's farm equipment was sprinkled and scattered, I wasn't paying attention to how or where I was driving. I was moving fast cross-country, picking up speed, and watching the grasshoppers jump as I created new paths through the tall summer weeds. My hair was flying in my face, making my ride even more uncontrolled. I didn't care. I was out, out in the air, struggling to find myself and any resemblance of the life I had before.

Bam! FUCK! Suddenly, the Ranger came to a crashing stop. I hit something, and I hit it hard! I flew up off the seat, my right arm collided with the steering wheel, and I fell back, hitting the seat as if I had just jumped in. My heart was beating faster than I had felt in a long time. It was the same sensation that comes over your body when you fall or hear really bad news. I was bewildered, sweaty, nervous, and scared. I started to cry. Uncontrollably. I had collided with a plow hidden underneath the grass and weeds. I never saw it. It wasn't there until I crashed into it.

I put the gear shift into reverse and gave it a little gas. It was still going! As I put it in drive, I looked down at my black, white, and tan check-patterned pants. I noticed wet, dark red spots. Then, feeling something on my right arm, I stretched it out in front of me, twisting my right hand inward, so I could see what I was feeling. It was my elbow! Something was sticking out of my arm, through the skin. It was white, pulpy, and bloody. I wasn't sure if it was bone or just the stuff that is inside your body that we never see.

You would think I would have driven slower and more cautiously considering what just happened with Momma, but I didn't. I needed medical attention, and I was sure I needed stitches. *Oh, no! What if it's broken?* I hadn't had a broken arm since I was twelve years old when I had fallen off my horse one summer, and needless to say, it was the hottest summer. I can remember having that cast on my arm for months and months.

All I could do was say a quick prayer, but I wasn't sure if God was really there. I wasn't sure if there even were a God anymore. I felt forgotten, like a piece of a puzzle that is never found. You can spend all your time searching, but you may never find it until you let go and just let it find you. I was learning that life was moving on, but I didn't feel I had direction or purpose. The one constant in my life had become chaos. I was lost. I was searching anywhere and everywhere to find myself, to find Momma, to find hope again.

In the same town where Momma was awaiting her funeral, I went to the emergency room and received nine stitches in my elbow. The doctor advised me to keep my arm in the same position as they wrapped it so I wouldn't break the stitches. This would prove impossible during visitation services. I think I hugged at least four hundred people without a second thought to my elbow, resulting in another visit to the ER that same night for more stitches.

Looking back on this, I believe God was answering pressing questions that I had:

Did Momma suffer?
Did it hurt?
Did she know?

I never felt any pain when my arm split wide open. It was instantaneous. I never had even one sensation, not a thing. I only felt scared and upset afterward. For

Momma, her afterward was heaven. You don't feel pain there, so I felt a little relief in hoping she went as quickly as I busted my elbow. Momma had left this earth, this earth filled with plows under weeds just waiting to devour us.

No matter what the cause of the death is, the way we react or don't react to it determines whether we are in a state of grief or complicated grief.

Recognizing the signs is crucial in getting to the next step. The step we do not want or feel like taking, but the step that we must take. It is important to remember that we are still here, and what a dismal and sad realization this can be. Believe me, I'm not putting this information in here so that you immediately feel cured. I'm putting this information in here for you to be better informed to help yourself or others you love who may be suffering. It's not normal. Forget the "new normal" phrase. That is out! This is different.

Here are some examples of the way it feels to have complicated grief:

> You think so much about the loss that it's hard to do nor-
> mal, everyday things that used to be second nature . . .
> such as taking good care of others, including children,
> going to work or concentrating at work, cooking, shop-
> ping, paying bills, and exercising.

> You find that memories of a loved one are upsetting, and
> it's reassuring to be upset because it means you are not
> moving on and leaving your loved one behind.

You feel like running away, even though this doesn't make sense and you know it's not the way to deal with difficult situations—doing this even if you are a person who usually faces problems and figures them out.

You do "crazy" things to try to escape from the pain, such as almost pretending the person is still here—asking questions over and over, continuing to do things you did when your loved one was sick, obsessing over how many places to set at the table, keeping their clothes and other possessions ready for them, and continuing to make the deceased person's favorite meals.

I suffered from every one of these examples. I would become upset with loved ones who didn't feel like talking about her, thinking that they were just forgetting her. *How could they?* I am the person who faces problems, as mentioned, so why did I want to turn away and run as fast as I could until my legs buckled beneath me or until I crashed?

According to The Center for Prolonged Grief at Columbia University, there are three key processes entailed in adapting to a loss:

1) accepting the reality, including the finality and consequences of the loss,

2) reconfiguring the internalized relationship with the deceased person to incorporate this reality, and

3) envisioning ways to move forward with a sense of purpose and meaning and possibilities for happiness.

I can't stress enough the importance of talking with a professional counselor, therapist, group therapist, psychiatrist, or psychologist during your time of pain. Everyone is going to give you their opinion of what you should do. Don't listen to them—*listen to you*! Be careful and use discernment when receiving the unsolicited advice of family, friends, and everyone in between. It can become overwhelming to take in all the information that well-intentioned people want to give you. As Gale said over and over to me, "Be gentle with yourself. Don't put too much pressure on yourself. This is a time to be particularly kind to yourself and say the words you need to say."

Resources

The Columbia Center for Complicated Grief

Complicated Grief—Symptoms and causes—Mayo Clinic

Psychiatry.org—Prolonged Grief Disorder

The Grief Experience: Survey Shows It's Complicated (webmd.com)

Sex, Grief, Anxiety, Depression, Trauma—Center for Growth Therapy (thecenterforgrowth.com)

Complicated Grief Therapy | Center for Complicated Grief (Columbia.edu)

Think Points

☐ Say the word. If it's *fuck*, say it. If it's *damn*, say it. Don't be afraid to let go of your emotions through your words. And if it's silence, that's something you can say too.

☐ If you are not comfortable saying it, write it. Writing is my outlet for my innermost thoughts and feelings. It is where I heal. Just get a piece of paper or your phone and write or type it. You may go back to this one day and see how far you've come in your healing process. You may even write a book of your own!

....

....

....

....

....

....

....

....

....

....

....

....

....

....

....

5

The Ring

Let yourself feel anything you want to
feel and anything you don't.
—Theo Boyd

WHEN I COULD SLEEP, it was a luxury I felt I didn't deserve, almost a guilt I would carry like a backpack filled with bricks. My mother was gone. My esteem was crushed. I felt unworthy of anything life had to offer because she couldn't enjoy these things anymore. I couldn't see my future without her, much less try to sleep. I was a painter with a bucket of black paint holding the biggest brush my hand could grasp. I colored everything I saw, felt, or thought with deep, heavy brush strokes up and down, back and forth, paint dripping everywhere.

Everything I did before and would try to do again was coated with this sticky, tarlike paint, and every day I applied a new coat. As much as my body fought against it, I would eventually set the brush down, and sleep would come.

For the first time in my life, no one was there to notice if I was tired, stressed, or falling apart. All the things my momma would notice. Now it was just me having to learn self-awareness, emotional maintenance, and self-talk for the first time.

The replay of her words connects with what I say to myself and confirms that she is with me. *Oh, Thelizabeth, you look tired. Don't overdo. You need to rest. Just lie down, and you sleep.* And it's not just the words; it is the timing of the words, the perfect timing. Her keen understanding of my condition in every moment of my life still awes me. She would see right through me. *How did she know what I was feeling at any given moment?* I would like to say that is just what mothers do, but her awareness was different. She saw what most never do. She may have lost her hearing as a baby, but she gained an insight into the souls of people, a gift of knowing more than you know about yourself. It happened time and time again throughout my life.

It was April 27, 1999, and I was taking my daughter, Reagen, to her first day of a new babysitting arrangement that would end up lasting five wonderful years. Momma was going to meet me in Hillsboro so that she could watch her while I went to work.

I was self-employed as a mortgage loan officer at the time and finding a babysitter or daycare that I was comfortable with had been very difficult. After several discussions back and forth, my parents had agreed to start helping, and we would "see how it goes." Despite the one-hour drive each way, Momma was the only person whom I felt comfortable leaving my precious baby girl with.

In Texas, everything is spaced out—acreage, roads, towns. We had space, sometimes too much space. Our family farm was located about fifteen minutes west of Hillsboro, near Whitney, population of about two thousand. Our farm was right on the line between Hillsboro and Whitney, with a Hillsboro phone number and a Whitney address making for easy access to either town. There was an outlet mall located off I-35 that would be a perfect place to meet.

When the mall was built in 1989, I remember how excited Momma was. She finally had a place to shop, and it was close enough to visit without being gone an entire day. Hillsboro had a rising population, but the outlet mall was declining. In the years to come, fewer of its stores would stay open.

When I was growing up, all Hillsboro had was a small Walmart, a Perry's (which is a small "everything" store), an Eckerd pharmacy, and a few locally owned grocery stores. I was always familiar with the grocery stores of each town because I would go with Daddy on scorching summer days to peddle our watermelons and cantaloupes. *Peddle* was a word I heard often. It's when we would go from store to store to sell the produce we had from a fresh crop—that is what *peddle* means. You never wanted to take for granted that just because you had a good relationship with a particular produce manager, you would be able to sell to him on any given day, no matter how ripe and delicious your fruit looked and tasted. When the mall came to town, a quick drive to "go to the grocery store" could easily turn into a stop at Casual Corner, DressBarn, or the Kitchen Collection.

I made the plan to meet Momma in the southside parking lot in front of Casual Corner. She drove their single cab, tan Chevrolet Silverado pickup truck, and as always, was there waiting when I pulled up. It was about 9:00 in the morning, and she would meet me back there at 5:00. I pulled up in the parking space to the left of her. Momma jumped out, opened the back passenger door of my maroon Nissan Pathfinder, and immediately started talking to Reagen. She lifted the carrier out of its base with Reagen inside, while I walked around and began transferring everything to her truck. She was filled with joy and smiles and light. Her make-up and hair were perfect as if she were going out shopping and to lunch, not watching a baby all day.

She wanted nothing more than to have this day, to drive the truck with Reagen by her side, and take her back to the farm. She wanted Reagen all to herself. I know Daddy was waiting back at home to greet them, coming in from the field for lunch and anticipating his granddaughter's first long visit alone with them.

When I say her awareness was different from others, this day came to mind. After the transfer was made, I laid the diaper bag on the floorboard below, kissed Reagen bye, and shut the passenger door on the pickup. I quickly hugged Momma as she slowly brushed her palm down my arm to slow me down a little. She said, "Today she is three months old, but one day you will look up, and she will be grown. Just slow down and enjoy it. It will go by so fast."

She knew I was stressed by all that being a mom is. She knew. No one else noticed, or if they did, they didn't take time to offer any advice for self-care. *How did she know to calm me and that Reagen was three months old already? Wasn't I supposed to be keeping up with her monthly birthdays?* I didn't, but she did, and she knew I needed to hear the words "slow down and enjoy it" because it did go by too fast. Gone. In a flash, everything became a memory.

I spent the first night after the accident with Daddy. Little did I realize it at the time, but that would be the first night of two months of nights that I stayed with Daddy. Daddy's guilt weighed heavy with his grief.

This first night, my husband and daughter stayed in the guest room. I did my best to shield them from Daddy's screams. I passed by the door a few times to peek in, and it seemed they were resting. I knew we would all need our rest in the coming days so at least some of us could be lucid in a time of pure pandemonium. This was the first night of my new reality. With no children living at home and me still on summer break from teaching, I knew I was the one.

The seconds, minutes, and early hours of July 30, 2019, were the most agonizing I have ever endured. There was no sleep, only lying down and listening to Daddy cry, scream, and call for her while he reached over to me, hugging me and imagining I was her. "Sue! Sue! Is that you? What have I done? Oh, my God, what have I done?" And the gut-wrenching sobs. This played out every night for about one month. And each night I grew stronger, or maybe I just grew more numb.

For almost fifty years, he had reached over and touched Momma lying there beside him. They had their special sign language in the dark. He shared how they would communicate with each other in the night to say everything was okay, connecting with a touch on the arm or leg.

At night, Momma took her hearing aid off. Daddy would reach over and lightly touch her arm, and she, his.

Death had stolen this from him. Darkness and nighttime became a brutal reminder of what once was. Half of his soul was gone. The body that lay beside him was mine, and that was hard for him to make sense of. It was for me too.

That first night and the following nights of that week, my thoughts were racing and chasing one another . . .

What happened?

How did it happen?

How would any of us ever get through this?

Sleep, I decided, wasn't a necessity anymore. I was scared of so many things now, and sleep had become one of them.

Sleeping represented two things—an escape from the pain and knowing that when I woke up, a more intense pain would be there to take its place. If I allowed myself the luxury of sleep, I felt I was cheating by turning off my body, losing my ability to feel, I was leaving her behind or forgetting her. I couldn't leave and go to a place where she wouldn't be thought of every second. That wasn't fair.

I was afraid to go to sleep and dream about her. Dreams are a cruel trick your mind plays on you, time and time again. I could try to sleep, but my mind was like that of another person, sitting there waiting to replay past movies, and I had a front-row seat. She was always beautiful and had the lead role, and I would wake up with a face wet from tears, imagining she was still here. *Did she want to hear about my dream?* I wish it hadn't ended, her movie, and I wish we were still writing its acts and watching it together.

Sleeping meant leaving her, watching her, and waking up without her. Sleep had manifest itself into an ongoing debate. Which was worse—denying myself sleep or allowing myself to see and feel her again in my dreams, only to come back to a reality that punched me hard in the gut? I had two disturbing and troublesome choices.

When sleep did force itself on me, I recall waking up, and all seemed good for the first few seconds. My mind would hear Momma in the kitchen cooking breakfast. She always had a certain energy about her, like the Energizer Bunny, but with the delicate touch of Caroline Ingalls or Olivia Walton. She was always doing something, day after day, morning after morning, night after night, and there was always breakfast. It was there on the table waiting for me when I woke up, or she was standing at the stove cooking, sipping on her tiny glass of cold orange juice.

Each morning seemed to be another ordinary day back at home with Momma and Daddy. I lay in bed, closed my eyes that had only opened to see it was morning, smelled the bacon frying, and heard the hot eggs popping in the skillet from the tiny air pockets of grease underneath. The oven door creaked as it opened and then closed quickly, only to check the browning on the biscuits. I could smell it, hear it, and even taste it, but it wasn't real. Nothing was. Not this morning. She was gone. And there was no breakfast.

Where was she? I wandered through her kitchen, but she wasn't there. I was still looking for her and was confused. When the realization finally came that there had been an accident, I still didn't know what was happening, where I was, or why I had woken up there, in Momma and Daddy's bed, on her side. My thoughts and emotions were foggy and desperately trying to catch up with this runaway train.

As I lay in their bed, with my eyes barely open, I saw a blurred figure of something leaning in the corner of the room facing me. Bulky and slouched over, this silhouette waited anxiously for me to wake up. One leg bent, with its foot sunk and heel bouncing up and down into where the two walls meet, arms crossed in front, sitting on big, gloved hands, just a foggy figure with a scowl for a face. It was hard to make out, so I closed my eyes tighter than before, hoping it would leave the room. Soon after, I felt its punch. I saw a figure of what seemed to be Mohammed Ali, Mike Tyson, and Sylvester Stallone, all rolled into one but with an anger about them that couldn't be satisfied. The climax of every fight or boxing match I had ever watched played out in an auto-replay, and no one could hit the Stop button. It didn't even wait for me to get out of bed. It knew when I was awake, and my mind was beginning to clear; whether I was lying flat or standing up didn't matter. BOOM! PUNCH to the gut! I immediately felt nauseous, wrapped my arms around my curled legs, tucked my chin into my chest, and squeezed my eyes shut again, much tighter than before. Under the covers is where I felt the safest. I whispered to myself, *Please stop. Please stop. Momma, make it go away.* Most days, I could catch my breath after a few moments. Other days took longer. *Momma, I can't do this. I can't be on this earth without you. Please make it stop.*

Our mothers are always there to shield us from pain, but mine was gone. I was alone in the ring—alone with this image with its devastating blows and distaste for me or life of any kind. This image represented everything I was feeling, thinking, or imagining. The boxer was the dark side of life—sin, the devil, and death—coming to see me every morning. It wasn't going to quit until I decided to stand up for myself and face this figure, this terrifying nightmare. It still punches me now, but I'm learning to punch back.

It was as if I had a newborn baby. I averaged about four hours of rest per night. It was hard to sleep, and when I did, a dream or nightmare was waiting for me. And the dread of what was waiting for me when I awoke was almost too much to bear.

I had the most phenomenal mother on the planet, and I think her superpowers took a while to transfer to me. Maybe they got lost for a short time in the universe as she traveled away. The important thing to remember is that I finally felt them trickle down to me. From her spirit into mine—she is here, alive, and lighting me up from the inside out. The hits still hurt, the fighter still fights, but it doesn't cripple me. I know how to hit back with my memories, the stories, the truths that only I can tell.

After many long months, I was eventually able to sleep better. I would wake up and see the boxer in the corner and feel the hit, but it didn't knock me down as it once did. I was starting to learn how to live a life that included this new counterpart and use the energy it created to power through the trying days ahead.

I thought this would be the last of it, but God had other plans. I tried to finish this book many times, but life gave me unexpected obstacles and more heartache. Soon the boxer would be hitting hard again, and those hits would drop me to my knees. I didn't realize it then, but God knew this story wasn't finished. Momma never did anything without Daddy, and Daddy never did anything without Momma. Daddy longed to be with Momma, in life, in spirit, and in this book.

Their story wasn't finished.

Think Points

How do you slow down and enjoy the little moments in your life?

....

....

....

....

....

....

....

....

....

....

....

....

What does your sleep look like, then and now?

....

....

....

....

....

....

....

....

....

....

....

....

6

Joe

*And we know that all things work together
for good to them that love God, to them who
are the called according to his purpose.*
—Romans 8:28

DADDY WAS ONE OF the most unforgettable characters you could ever meet. With his lean frame, standing six feet, four inches tall; his brown hair perfectly combed; eyes tinted in the softest powder blue—he was made to stand out among the rest, matching all the ingredients in the tall, dark, and handsome cliché. His farmer's tan, which stretched down his arms and around his neck, subtly faded to a V-shape at the top of his chest where his T-shirts would lay. With Daddy, it was all about the charisma, the spell. He had the ability to captivate anyone he was interacting with. It was like watching Elvis, but without the dancing and music. He was hypnotizing. He was my daddy.

"I'm just a homeboy," he would say, and there's never been a truer statement.

Daddy was born in a small farmhouse on December 19, 1943, by the wood stove. At the same time he was coming into this world, his older brother was on a bus heading toward World War II. Daddy was the baby of the family, with two older sisters and one older brother. Joe Bob received extra attention from his position in the birth order of this small, farming, Christian family. My grandmother had prayed daily that her little baby, Joe Bob, would one day become a preacher.

And he did.

My grandmother, Lillie Elizabeth Boyd, or Meme—what I called her—was a spiritual rock. Her faith could not be moved, and her beliefs on the Bible and its truths were steadfast. "The Bible says it, I believe it, and that settles it" were the words she lived by. I can vividly remember hearing her sweet, but strong voice as she cooked a hamburger for me on her small gas cookstove in the old farmhouse located across from our house. I would get off the school bus only to be faced with an immediate dilemma. *Do I go to Meme's really quick for an after-school snack, or do I get home?* Meme's house always won, although Momma would soon be looking for me.

Meme's hamburgers were the best I have had or will ever eat. It wasn't the bread or meat—it was the love of God that shined through her, trickling down to me through her simple, juicy, buttery, toasted, and unforgettable hamburgers. Delicious! It was in this farmhouse that great food was made and where my daddy was born. It was farm-to-table style every day. The meat came from our cows, the eggs from our chickens, the vegetables from our gardens, and our cups were filled from the love in the preparations—constant, deep, and never-ending. They were overflowing. One of the sweetest things I've ever known is the love shared in this house.

Daddy was a son, uncle, husband, father, speaker, teacher, preacher, farmer, and rancher. Whew! He was my everything. He was a hero to many, but especially to me. I'm a daddy's girl and always will be.

In high school, Daddy was very well-liked and loved by many. He was just one of those good guys. You know, the good ones who care, who love, who protect, who understand, who listen, and who save. Yes, he brought many people to the Lord through his ministry as a preacher at Bethel Bible Church for thirty-three years. Having only taught himself the scriptures, with a little help from Meme, of course, Joe Bob was "the most educated, self-taught individual of the Bible," as many seminary scholars would say. He devoured the Bible from age nine. He couldn't get enough of it. He knew so much that he became dangerous—well, I mean only in the sense of playing a Bible trivia game. We never had a chance. He knew all the answers, and there was no beating him. On the flip side, Daddy could shed the Sunday suit, put on his Levi jeans, Redwing boots, a denim work shirt Momma had just pressed, and his International Tractor cap, and be covered in sand within minutes.

Daddy was a farmer of Spanish peanuts, and they were our main source of income. Cattle, watermelons, cantaloupe, and preaching came second. My granddaddy had been a peanut farmer too. Our soil was perfect for them and a requirement. Sandy loam, it's called. Daddy loved the sand, the dirt, and everything that came from it. Momma would remind him to "leave it on the porch." Sand was as common on the floors in our house as the black-eyed peas cooking on the stove.

In 1970, Daddy was drafted in the lottery to go to Vietnam and fight in a war he didn't understand. The day before he was to leave, a friend of my grandfather's told Daddy he should apply for an agricultural deferment. "We need farmers to stay home." Daddy applied, knowing that God was showing him a way to stay with Momma and keep working the farm they had just started. He got it! He was deferred for the purpose of agriculture, farming, and ranching.

Daddy's purpose was in the land, the farm. He was born in it, and although people say don't let things define you, farming defined Joe Bob Boyd. Daddy was the Charles Ingalls of Hill County, Texas. The land meant something to him, and it held his heart. "I know every centimeter of this place." He would even scoop up dirt or a rock, wrap it, and take it as a gift for people who were having a momentous anniversary or birthday. It brought them to tears because it was the land they grew up on. Something as simple as a rock or some dirt would bring back a flood of childhood memories. And if it was a really special occasion, they would get an arrowhead from his collection. He probably had about one thousand that he'd found over the years in the land.

Daddy loved people. I remember the stories Daddy would tell me about his childhood. Like fairy tales, they were soaked in friendship, love, and warmth—and they were true! I felt like I was listening to a collection of Norman Rockwell paintings come to life. Daddy's friends were as loyal as the dogs he had through the years, and in that same respect, never forgotten. From best friends to his girlfriends, he had them all. And his girlfriends were just that, girl *friends*. He had as many female friends as male friends. He knew how to talk to anyone, boy or girl, old or young.

In Daddy's early years, he attended a country school. It was a one-room schoolhouse, similar to the church on the *Little House on the Prairie* television series. During the week, it was a schoolhouse, and on Sundays, it was church. Daddy said he got in trouble numerous times at that country school for either getting his clothes dirty or not wanting to let the girls play ball with the boys. What he loved most was that he didn't have to wear shoes to the country school. He would recall the days and smile with complete joy when he told us about his youth. These early childhood experiences shaped and molded the man that would later lead a community.

Daddy was funny. He used humor in almost all of what life gave him. He could make us laugh with his quick comebacks and original jokes. He was a writer. He would write complete comedy skits.

The House That Was So Small . . .
- the mailbox could only hold envelopes vertically.
- the refrigerator door opened in.
- you could only eat half a foot-long hotdog.
- the shower could only hold half a bar of soap.
- you had to sleep standing up.

Daddy was always making us laugh, everyone. His classmates from high school and college said he kept them "in stitches." He did so many things through the years that I find myself doing now, like memorizing the back of the Crest toothpaste tube. He would also write to companies if their products were defective or lacking. He wrote to Campho-Phenique once because the tiny paper cap on the inside of the screw top would come off and not stay where it was supposed to. They responded. He received two cases of Campho-Phenique and "every damn one of them, the cap comes off."

He wrote poetry, short stories, sermons, speeches, and just about everything. He was a gifted writer and creator of ideas that were so original he would say, "Don't tell anyone." This was usually about his inventions. He had the most unique ideas for inventions:

- A toothbrush ball filled with toothpaste that you could chew like gum.
- Peanut butter and jelly already mixed together.
- A light with a fan on the other end, so you can see your book and keep cool at the same time.

It seems like someone gave away his secrets because these "inventions" of Daddy's have all come to fruition.

Joe Bob was a pillar of his community. As a minister, he preached at weddings and funerals and prayed at almost any event I attended. He was the strength. He took on this role and didn't realize it would take so much of him. He was there for everyone. I worried often through the years that he did so much for everyone else that he wasn't doing enough for himself.

Daddy knew his limits, but he gave beyond them. He gave others hope, which gave him purpose. He got his energy from others. It was a fuel that powered him to take charge, lead, and be an example that most can only aspire to. He did.

"Be a Christian," he would say before I would leave the house for school, dates, work—anything, and although as a teenager, I acted like it bothered me, I remembered it. It's advice that I have taken with me throughout my life.

One of Daddy's favorite movies, *Steel Magnolias*, says it best:

Laughter through tears is my favorite emotion.
—Truvy, played by Dolly Parton
(also one of Daddy's favorites)

Daddy had a series of health issues that seemed to come as quickly as the clouds turn to twisters in late spring. In 2006, Daddy was diagnosed with prostate cancer. He caught it early and had a prostatectomy in 2007. Later in 2009, Daddy had the first of several mini-strokes that would continue through the years. He had a stent procedure for an artery in his heart that was partially blocked, and he was on blood pressure and blood-thinner medications. He stopped being as active as he once had been. He was a farmer. He worked hard building fences, working cattle, plowing fields, fixing tractors, and hoeing fields of peanuts, watermelons, cantaloupe, and everything else we grew on the farm. In heat that would suffocate most people, Daddy was treading through the sandy soil pulling, picking, and peddling. "My body's shot," he began to say.

I look at this now as just one more sacrifice that farmers make to bring food to our tables. A farmer's work is never done, and the toll that work takes on their health is greater than what most consumers realize. Farmers pay a price, the price of life.

We started to see a change in Daddy, but it was gradual. I began to notice his short-tempered outbursts with the smallest of things. He would get frustrated if Momma got the mail from the mailbox too late each day or if she picked from the wrong turnip plants in their garden.

Not being able to farm the land, run the cattle, and jump the fences anymore made Daddy feel like a box of old puzzle pieces stuck in a closet. It's hard to have hope when your purpose begins to fade or diminish in ways beyond your control.

I told many close friends and family at Momma's visitation, "When Momma died, Daddy died too." I felt like I lost both of my parents on that day.

Think Points

☐ Is there a small item that is a big memory for you, like sand or a rock was for Daddy?

....

....

....

....

....

....

....

....

....

☐ How can you support someone in grief? Daddy always thought of others, and he told me that when you do something for someone else, that is when you start to feel better.

....

....

....

....

....

....

....

....

....

....

....

7

Peanut Shells

*God may give you more than you can
handle, but it is still part of his plan.*
—Theo Boyd

I WAS A DADDY'S GIRL for fifty years. I looked up to him more than any other man in my life. It would be hard for any future male figures in my life to make the grade and measure up to my Daddy's excellence; he was my gauge. I remember so many things about him, so many things that are part of who I am. It was difficult to decide what to include in this book and what I could save for the next one.

Daddy walked tall, loved all, and, well—he loved peanuts. It's that simple. He farmed them, shelled them, ate them, and they were always around. Momma made peanut butter, peanut brittle, peanut patties, chocolate-covered peanuts, and anything else you can imagine to be cooked, boiled, baked, or fried using peanuts. Peanuts were as much a part of our life as Jesus and Johnson grass.

He kept a can of Planters Redskin Spanish Peanuts on his nightstand for a convenient late-night snack, and there were usually several back-up cans in the pantry. He also kept bags of the bigger peanuts, still in their shell, near his bedside. He loved to crack them with his teeth and eat the salty peanuts inside. I was always finding peanut shells around the house, usually along Daddy's trail to the kitchen and bathroom.

When he was farming peanuts, the fresh ones couldn't be beat. "It's a good thing I didn't have a peanut allergy," I would say jokingly to Daddy. "Yep, guess I would've had to farm somethin' else," he would reply.

Fall was his favorite time of year, and I know why. It was harvest time and soon to be a time of rest. He could spend more time with us and less time with the tractors and sand. The sky turned from a distinct summer blue to a softer sepia shade as the sand from the fields would linger in the air until nightfall. I can remember the smell as I stepped off the school bus in the afternoons. As soon as my feet hit the dirt, the breeze would pass by and through my hair. I would take in a breath, and the harvest scent was strong. We didn't need fancy candles to take us to a season we all loved; we could just step outside.

Momma would take me with her to help Daddy combine the peanuts. A combine is the machine we used, pulled by the tractor, to take the dried peanut plants off the ground and shake them, discarding the plant back onto the ground and sending the peanuts in their shells to the big bucket, or hopper, on top. My favorite part was watching the filled bucket of our old red combine rise up and pour out into one of Daddy's peanut trailers. Sometimes, if I was patient, he would let me sit on the huge mound that had already been dumped into the trailer, and very carefully let the bucket pour out a few more next to me, creating a small peanut shower. I would pretend it was raining peanuts, and I was the peanut princess.

I was his princess.

He was my daddy.

He was.

I ache writing this because I didn't share much of this book with him. I wish I had read some parts of this book to Daddy and asked for his advice. He knew I was writing a book on grief, my grief, and that I wanted to help others, but I knew I couldn't help him. No one could. The weight of the accident and his role in it became too much. I had intentionally not talked much about what I was writing because I didn't want him to hurt anymore. I didn't want him to read some of the things I am sharing with you.

I wish I had held him more and told him how thankful I was for having a daddy as wonderful as he was. I wish I had told him every day how much I loved him and how I never blamed him, not ever. When others had the luxury of silencing their grief with blame, I never did, nor did I ever want to. It was an accident, plain, pure, and simple. A horrible, tragic accident—all of it, from beginning to end. His best friend and the love of his lifetime was gone, and he felt responsible. The weight of that was more than anyone could bear. It was more than he could bear.

Saturday, June 18, 2022.

My sister and I had spent lunchtime with Daddy, ate barbecue sandwiches, and gave him his Father's Day gifts. It had worked out better for everyone that we saw Daddy on that Saturday. This day was a good day.

We met at Daddy's house. Nellene greeted us at the door. She was Daddy's girlfriend for the last two years and was a godsend to us all, although I didn't always feel this way. I wasn't pleased with their relationship at first. I didn't want anyone in Momma's kitchen except Momma. When talking to Daddy on the phone, I could hear kitchen sounds in the background—plates being put away, spoons hitting the inside of a pot on the stove, glasses being set on the table. I hated hearing it because I knew it wasn't Momma. I was being forced to realize Momma was gone, again. My mind weighed reality against a fantasy I continued to play on a loop. Nellene was ruining it.

"She needs to leave," I would say in a harsh tone when talking to Daddy on the phone. "She is here because I want her to be. We are just friends, and I have missed having someone to talk to," Daddy would tell me. This didn't do much to change my thoughts, but at least it shut me up.

Looking back now, I realize that Daddy needed Nellene as much as I needed someone. It gets lonely being alone, imagine that.

Nellene has coarse, dark hair that always looks soft from being freshly brushed. She is a lady who knows who she is. She is comfortable in her skin. Whether she is doing a ton of yardwork or cooking a hearty, five-course meal, she carries herself with a proud, yet humble confidence. She is educated, not only from books and school, but from life experiences.

You know what Nellene is thinking and feeling at any moment, and she isn't embarrassed to talk to you about it. She gave Daddy a run for his money when it came to talking, and for Daddy, there was another reason she was so special to him. Her laugh. She has a warm and comfortable laugh that makes you feel that everything will be okay and nothing is worth being upset about. It has a calmness about it that we didn't realize we were missing.

Daddy loved to laugh, and he hadn't laughed much during the past three years. With Nellene, I heard Daddy laugh again. She was the perfect partner for him. Nellene was exactly what Daddy needed. She was what we all needed, and maybe she needed us too.

They grew up playing together and running through the same fields. Nellene was a country girl who knew the land, the community, the friends, and all those stories from their younger days. She and Daddy would spend time looking at old yearbooks and sharing stories of days gone by, jokes, songs, and a relationship that lasted a lifetime.

It was obvious to everyone that they loved each other, but it was a different kind of love—a caring kind. Daddy would always say, "I told Nellene I love her as a friend, but I will never love anyone like I love my Sue." That wedding band always remained on his hand. It never left.

My relationship with Nellene evolved into something sweet and unexpected. It's not always this way, so I was cautious at first. For me, for Daddy, for us, we were blessed that God gave us Nellene. She was like the favorite aunt whom you saw at Thanksgiving and Christmas, wondering how they could be so great and always wanting to be in their presence. She never attempted to take Momma's place, but she was there. She did what she never had to do.

I realize now that God put her in our path. She became and is still part of our family, but I think of her now as much more than a favorite aunt, more like a second mother.

We had a wonderful visit for Father's Day that Saturday, although Daddy couldn't get his barbecue sandwich box opened quick enough. He was frustrated. Daddy's dementia took away his patience factor and his filter for dealing with routine things. He was easily aggravated and frustrated. He was mostly sad and upset about who he felt he had become, a burden to others. "I'm pitiful," he would say. "I'm tired of living like this," he repeated quite often in the last few months. "Sue!" he would yell out randomly.

He had lost hope. I knew it wasn't a quality of life that anyone desires to live, one without hope. His memory was constantly playing the scene of when Momma died, and he is the only one who saw firsthand what exactly happened. The horrific tragedy that never left him was topped by the debilitating disease that was stealing what was left of his freedom.

But it was Father's Day the next day, and we were there because he was our daddy. My sister and I took pictures with him, gave him some gifts, and stayed a little while, until Daddy got too tired to stay in the kitchen with us. I had gone into Target the day before and grabbed him some comfy clothes—socks, pajamas, and loungewear. He opened them and smelled them.

Along with pleasant smells like a gift, Daddy didn't mind smelling unpleasant things. I remember once checking on the cattle, their feed, and their vitamin lick station—I guess that's what you call it. As we opened the barbed wire gate to drive into the pasture, we smelled something really bad. It was awful. It smelled like a field of rotten tomatoes mixed with a thousand dirty baby diapers. I had to hold my nostrils closed and breathe through my mouth, which was not even a better option, but Daddy wanted to check things out. Sure enough, the liquid vitamins had become rotten. This was a funny thing about Daddy. He loved to smell things—the good, the bad, and the ugly.

After opening and smelling his gifts, he said, "Thank you so much," and went to bed.

Did he know then?

Did he know those socks would never touch his feet?

Did he know he would never use the gifts I got for him?

Did he feel somewhat guilty about opening them, knowing they would never be used?

I had bought him a card with a picture of a dog on the front that looked like his dog, Barney. It was a funny card, and the inside message read, "I hope you know how much fun you bring to so many." I loved this card, and I knew Daddy would, too, but I lost it. That day, Saturday, while preparing to go to his house, I couldn't find it. I looked everywhere. I was running behind so I just stopped looking for it. I thought, *Well, I'll just take it to him later. I'll take it to Daddy, later.*

The day went well, and as I was leaving, I told Daddy I was going to church the next morning. I asked if he wanted me to pick him up to go, and he said, "No!" rather emphatically. I knew he didn't want to go, and quite honestly, he couldn't.

I was becoming more concerned with Daddy's declining mobility and what the white matter disease was doing to him. It was basically crippling him a little more each day from the inside out, as was his grief. He didn't have the strength to get out of bed most days, and he longed to go back to bed when he had been up for only the time it took to eat a small meal. "I want to go back to bed," he would say in a childlike voice. He was tired. "Plain tired," as he would write later in his last note.

I stood in the doorway to his bedroom, looking at him on the bed, as I had so many times over the past three years. I knew he was miserable, emotionally and physically, and completely tired of life and what it had offered him. But he was there. He was right there, always.

"I love you, Daddy. Happy Father's Day."

"I love you, too, Thelizabeth. You'll never know how much."

Leaving the house that day, I didn't know that would be the last time I would see Daddy, alive.

It had been a big day, and I had church the next morning. I practiced a couple of the hymns on the piano, "Blessed Assurance" and "How Great Thou Art," two of Daddy's favorites. I was ready for the next day, and it was time to go to sleep. I got in bed and closed my eyes. My dog, Manly, was lying at my feet.

As I was closing my eyes to drift off, the strangest sensation came over me. I was in our old farmhouse. I was young again. I felt the breeze coming through the windows in Momma and Daddy's bedroom and traveling through the house. I heard the sound of the doorknob that separated the kitchen and dining room from their bedroom. The door was a pale yellow color with paint chips on either side from years of wear. I kept opening and closing the door, feeling the layers of peeling paint on my fingertips and how the round fixture fit inside my palm. I opened my eyes. *What was this?* I wasn't asleep. I wasn't dreaming. I was awake, but I was somewhere else when I closed my eyes.

I didn't want it to be over. I hadn't felt this before. I was so happy and calm, and for once, I was breathing so deeply and effortlessly that I was becoming tired. I closed my eyes again, hoping to go right back there. I did. I was dreaming while I was wide awake.

I reached to close the door while it creaked as the spring bounced in place. I reached out again, closing my hand on the doorknob, and the door opened again with the same sensation. This was a feeling I remembered. The smells, the air, the love—it was all back.

I opened my eyes, looking at Manly and the television I hadn't turned off yet. I closed my eyes again, and we were all there—Momma, Daddy, my sister, and me. *How was this feeling coming to me?* I questioned it, but I didn't fight it. I smiled, feeling all the love again. I smiled, seeing Daddy at his rolltop desk studying, seeing Momma in the kitchen putting the meringue on one of her chocolate pies, and me, soaking it all up and hoping that they knew I was there. "Hi, Momma and Daddy. I love you. What are y'all doing? Why are we here?" I said out loud. I opened and closed the door again and again. I heard Daddy. I couldn't make out the words, but I could hear his voice.

He was home again.

I opened my eyes and looked at the clock on my nightstand. It was 12:30 a.m.

I fell into a deep sleep.

June 19, 2022.

The next morning, I woke up. It was Father's Day, the third one without Momma. Remembering the feeling from the night before, I lay in the covers. Manly was waking up and licking my arm, his sign to get me up and take him on his routine walk. I couldn't explain what I had felt the night before, but I hoped I would feel it again. I never told anyone about this, until now.

I got up, brushed my teeth, and had plenty of energy for my day. I slept well! I was getting my songbook and Bible ready for church, and the card I had bought Daddy for Father's Day fell out onto the floor. I found it, or it found me. Instead of our usual walk, I decided to take Manly out to Daddy's house so he could run there on the farm, and I could give Daddy the card. Not only that—I could surprise Daddy with breakfast.

As Manly and I made our way to the farm, I texted Shari. I was going to meet her to go to church that morning.

I had just enough time to grab breakfast, get to Daddy, let Manly run, and get back to get dressed for church. Whew! It was already shaping up to be a busy morning.

"Can I get a big breakfast with hotcakes, extra bacon, sausage, a medium black coffee, and a large black coffee?"

Two coffees—one for me, one for Daddy. I usually didn't eat breakfast, but I loved to drink coffee with Daddy and watch him enjoy his.

After I picked up the breakfast, I was on my way. I turned down the gravel driveway, as I had done a million times. I parked in my usual spot under the horse apple tree that offered much shade on a hot summer day. This day was shaping up to be "a scorcher," as Daddy would say. I grabbed the McDonald's sack and the two coffees and made my way into the house. We didn't lock the back door anymore, so if Daddy needed help, he could hit the button on his emergency necklace and first responders or one of us could easily get to him.

Barney met me at the door and brushed past me so fast without hesitation. I knew he probably needed to go to the bathroom. Daddy wasn't able to let him out anymore as much as one should. Barney met Manly outside, and they did their normal chasing of the cats and cattle.

"Good morning, Daddy. Happy Father's Day!" I hollered out. I knew he might be sleeping, so I didn't worry much when he didn't respond.

I made my way down the hallway to his bedroom, my parents' bedroom. I looked to the left into where Daddy lay on his bed. His right leg was hanging off the bed, but I didn't think too much about it. For some reason, I didn't make it into the kitchen. I immediately turned into his room and went to Momma's side of the bed, as Daddy's leg was somewhat blocking me from getting close enough to wake him.

"Daddy? Daddy? Wake up." I set the breakfast down on Momma's nightstand. I looked over at Daddy. I saw blood on his eyes. My immediate thought was that he had fallen and made his way back to the bed and was lying there unconscious from the fall. I touched his shoulder, then his hands that were on his chest. They seemed cold, but he wasn't covered up so I thought he was just cold from lying there hurt. "Daddy! Daddy! Daddy! Are you okay? Okay, I'm going to get help!"

I left the bedroom, ran back down the hallway into the garage, and was trying to get my cell phone. Daddy had a landline, but for some reason, I raced to get my cell phone. As I ran from the garage into the yard, I fell. My knees buckled, and I lost my strength. I got up fast and dusted the gravel from my legs and the insides of my palms, and I made my way to get my phone.

I hit each number very carefully, 911, and waited. A lady answered, "Nine-one-one, what is your emergency?"

I gave her the address very slowly and carefully.

"My name is Theo Boyd. My daddy is Joe Bob Boyd. Hurry! He is unresponsive. There is blood on his face. I think he fell. He's on blood thinners, and he may be bleeding out. He's not answering me."

"Can you tell me your address one more time?" As she calmly asked me question after question, I felt as if I were in a bad dream where I'm on a game show, and no matter what I say, there's always another question. I repeated the address and our names. I also told her to hurry and that I wanted to hang up now and call my sister. I didn't want to be alone. I wanted help. I needed someone with me.

The operator wouldn't let me hang up. She asked me to go back to my dad and put the phone up to his ear. I refused, until she finally won. I don't know why I was so hesitant to go back in and do this. *Could my brain have already recorded what really happened and be protecting me?*

"Okay, I'm going in." I walked over to the same side of the bed where I first saw he had blood on his eyes, and I held the phone out to his left ear.

This time, I saw much more than I did the first time. I saw blood. I saw so much blood. It was in the shape of a large circle, the size of a yoga ball, and he was lying on top of it. I looked at his ear as I held the phone, and I couldn't find it. I couldn't find his ear. It was underneath a mountain of blood. I screamed, or at least I think I did.

"I'm hanging up now." And I did. I called my sister as I ran outside.

The sunshine was outside. I kept retreating from Daddy's bedside to the outside, to the light.

"Daddy! It's Daddy!!!! There is so much blood. Hannah! Daddy is hurt. Please come here!" I tried to explain the scene to my sister. "I think Daddy fell and he isn't waking up. I think he fell and there is blood all over. I am freaking out! Oh God! Oh God!"

My sister says that I was just screaming, and she could hardly understand me.

"Thelizabeth, Thelizabeth. It's okay. Listen to me. I'm so sorry, but you have to go back in there."

"NO! I'm not. I don't think I can. No, Hannah!"

"Thelizabeth, please. Remember, when Momma died, we wanted to know exactly what happened. You have to go back in and look for a gun."

It hadn't dawned on me until she said those words. *Daddy may have done this! Oh, my God, Daddy? Did you do this? Please, God, no!!!!!*

"Okay, will you stay on the phone with me?" I pleaded.

"Yes, of course. I'm here," Hannah assured me.

"Okay, I'm going in." The dogs were following me around outside, but they wouldn't come into the house for some reason. They were standing in the doorway from the garage into the house. They knew something.

I went to Daddy's side of the bed this time. I touched his leg, feeling it, cold and stiff. I attempted to move his leg over a little. "Daddy? Daddy? Daddy! Daddy! Oh, God, NO! I see the gun. His pistol. I see it!!!!!!!! There is a gun!"

There was a pistol on the bed, lying next to his right side. Both his hands were on his chest, neatly at rest. I didn't touch anything, except Daddy.

I could hear my sister saying, "I'm coming there. Thelizabeth, I'm on my way."

"It's okay, Daddy. It's okay. You're going to be okay." I just kept saying this over and over.

The next few minutes are blurry. I'm trying to recall everything, every second, but the mind will often block the images from trauma to protect itself. That is what happened here.

I was still waiting on the emergency people. I was walking in circles in the yard. I called Shari. She lived close by, and she could come be with me until someone got there. I don't remember what I said or how I said it. She came quickly. Once again, there we were. Three years later. I asked her to go in with me to make sure Daddy wasn't still alive. I kept doubting my eyes, my touch. She went with me. "Oh, Joe Bob." I looked at her for confirmation that he was really gone. She nodded yes.

I thought he may still be alive and just in need of blood and medical attention. Several people who showed up over the next several hours say that I was asking if my daddy was really dead. *Was he?* "Can you make sure that Daddy is not alive?" I asked the emergency workers, the sheriff, the funeral home people that came. "Are you sure he is dead?" "Is my daddy really gone?" "You can tell me; I can handle it."

The mind can definitely play tricks on you in grief. I was in complete disbelief that this was happening, another traumatic event, and my mind wasn't allowing me to move forward. It was creating alternative scenarios better than the reality in front of me. Imagining that Daddy was just hurt was a protection from the alarming certainty that he was dead.

A truck was approaching. We could hear it outside. Shari walked out of the room to go and meet whoever it was and show them in.

I stayed in with Daddy. I looked closer. I had to make sure I saw what I saw.

With Momma, there were so many questions that I will never be able to answer. I wanted to know what the scene looked like. I wanted to know if Momma was on her side, face down, looking up, and I just wanted to know exactly how she looked when she left us. With Daddy, I had no questions. I saw it all. I am so thankful for this moment.

I was the first one to see Daddy set free. Daddy was no longer a prisoner in his body and to his torturing thoughts. I went to Momma's side of the bed, soaking up the last moments I would be with Daddy in the house. No coffee, no breakfast, no conversation, but we were there, together.

I avoided the gun. I got up on the bed on my knees, I bent down to Daddy. I looked so closely. He was my daddy, and I wasn't scared to see anything anymore. This was the third time I had left and come back in, so my eyes and mind were allowing more to soak in. I looked down at the large circle of blood under his head and noticed something. I became curious and unafraid as I looked closely. Still, no one else was in the room. Not yet. I was in the few and most precious moments that many never get. These were my moments, the ones I had longed for with Momma. I had only my imagination of what had happened. This time, God was letting me in.

As I wiped the tears out of my eyes, I began to focus on something that had captured my attention on the bed. It was tiny and there were several, like little balls or specks of something. I looked around to make sure no one had come into the house or was watching me, as if I was about to do something wrong. I reached down to touch one, and I picked it up. It was a peanut shell. I reached for another—peanut shells! "Daddy!" I said out loud. I found these peanut shells, all covered in Daddy's blood. He had been eating peanuts in the bed, of course. Something so simple and enjoyable for him, but that he left here. I felt them in my fingertips one by one, rolling them back and forth. For me, it was proof of his existence and his contribution to the world. This man had been here. This man had made a difference. I smiled as the tears streamed down my face as fast as his blood must have poured out over them.

Daddy's favorite food to the very end, peanuts. This peanut farmer enjoyed what he had grown until his dying breath. Bless the farmer and his crop. This farmer. This man. Daddy.

He left my sister and me a note. I never saw it during the chaos. The sheriff brought it to me a few hours later. I was upset that I didn't see the note first. I wanted to be the one who saw everything this time. I needed to control something in the situation. Often our feelings of anger or jealousy are just our attempts at keeping control when everything around us is the opposite. When we do this, we are protecting ourselves from the unknown, the unthinkable, the unimaginable.

I grabbed it from the sheriff's hands and turned away from everyone. As their eyes followed me, I began to read it. Daddy's handwriting was similar to that of a serial killer's. I had self-published two short stories for Daddy over the past several years, and I told him that was one of the most difficult tasks I had ever faced. I would often text Momma and send her a picture of a word, waiting for Daddy to let us know what it was. The funny thing is, Daddy didn't know half the time. "My handwriting is getting so bad that I can't even read it." His chicken-scratch, quickly jotted down notes, and scattered stories across his desk were familiar topics for us to all laugh about.

Daddy had preached many suicide deaths over the years. He knew it would be important for law enforcement to know he was responsible for this, and no one was to blame. He was a very smart man who never stopped thinking of others. Even in a time when he was about to do the most unselfish and incomprehensible of all things, he thought of leaving us a note.

I still refer to Daddy's death as "the accident" because it happened only because of the accident on Monday, July 29, 2019, in which Momma died. I tell myself that Daddy committed "Sue-icide" because he needed to be with his Sue, Momma. And they are together again, after three long years, and the love remains.

I treasure his final note. I keep it in a place where all my special things are, and in that place deep inside the smallest corner of my heart. There are still a few words that I cannot decipher, but I will never stop trying. I will never stop trying to read every single last word he wrote.

It means the world to me. They were Daddy's last words, his last thoughts, and his last written letter.

I often tell people that God *can* give you more than you can handle, but that doesn't mean it's not still part of his plan. It is.

Think Points

This was such a hard chapter to write, so coming up with a Think Point was very difficult.

If I have to sum it up, I would say, "I have no idea what you are going through, but I want to be here for you by sharing this book and I hope you'll share with others who need it too."

I will share this book with ....
because...

....

....

....

....

....

....

....

....

....

....

....

....

....

....

....

....

The peanut farmer, Joe Bob Boyd, 2012.

8

Clouds

*This book is woven with weather—its
conditions and the mood it creates.
The Texas climate shaped my life—it set the
stage, the smells taking me back in time.*
—Theo Boyd

Farming and the weather go hand in hand. Morning, noon, and night, the weather is a constant concern. I told Daddy once that farming was like gambling: you never know the hand you'll be dealt. He didn't care for that comparison, but I still feel it's pretty accurate. Through the years, I learned that weather is the single most necessary ingredient for a farmer and as unpredictable as Sunday church attendance.

Daddy never missed a forecast. Atmospheric conditions were as important as carrying our Bibles to church. If you missed hearing the forecast, you might as well just forget about salvation. All hope was lost.

But if you did miss it, there was always someone on the road who wanted to talk for hours about the chances of rain or sun. I could write a book on the phrases concerning weather that are forever etched in my brain.

"Diju git inny rane?"

"How much rain diju git?"

"Whew! It's sure dry. We need a good rain."

"Boy howdy, it's gettin' hot!"

"God, please send us some rain."

"Man alive, it's wet out there. Can't get the plow in the field."

"School bus doesn't need to drive down that road—it'll get stuck."

"Creek may get out."

As I sit writing this, it's raining outside. When my grief began, it was hot, dry, and dusty. Another saying I heard from Daddy many times was, "August is just one of those months you suffer through." Little did we know at the time but suffering from the heat was no comparison to what we would endure in August 2019.

Momma's last week on earth, the weather was gorgeous. The days were cool, the mornings and evenings even cooler. The weather was very unusual for that time of year. We had low humidity, which always makes everyone happy, and as Momma would say, "The house just smells cleaner." When you can eliminate summer's humidity from the Texas air, everything is as crisp as one of Daddy's denim work shirts, starched and ironed by Momma, of course.

Momma and I texted each other several times that week about the weather and how much we were enjoying it. She told me she had been taking walks outside early in the morning and couldn't believe it was so cool. She said how nice it was to leave a few windows open early in the morning and get a fresh smell in the house. It reminded her of California.

When you know someone, you know what type of weather they like. Momma's was cool and cloudy. She loved days that were a little calmer than most. When it was sunny, expectations were higher, and work was harder. When clouds and rain came, she could rest and take the day off, at least from outside work. With cooler temperatures, she didn't have to listen to the buzz of the window units, which always covered up any other sounds she may need to hear.

She loved to recall her days living in California, how she would leave her window barely cracked each night, letting in a cool breeze with no mosquitos, no bugs, only pristine air. She said during the day you could wear a sweater or short sleeves. It didn't matter. They didn't have air conditioners because they didn't need them. I couldn't imagine it. *NO* air conditioners? Wow, that must have been something. Each time she talked about living in California, she smiled. I knew it was a part of a life she had before Daddy, me, or my sister, and I could tell she missed it.

In 1965, a few years after graduating from Itasca High School and attending Hill Junior College in Hillsboro, Texas, Momma got a job working as a nanny for a family living in Dallas. I will refer to the couple as Mr. and Mrs. A for the sake of privacy. She was in charge of their two-year-old son, Patrick. Shortly after she was hired, the family made plans to move to Hillsborough, California, and offered Momma the chance to move with them. She took it. When she would talk about it, we always thought it was funny that she left Hillsboro, Texas, to go to Hillsborough, California, which is spelled differently but sounds the same. She flew back and forth often to visit her parents, my grandparents, and Daddy. She loved flying. She would tell Daddy all about it, but he had no desire to fly anywhere. I could tell Momma would have loved any chance to get back on a plane again.

She made California her home for almost three years. I wish I had the exact dates, but I never sat and wrote down all the details, thinking she would always be here to ask. All details set aside, she loved her time there, and the weather was one of the main reasons. She said her hair was always perfect, and she never even broke a sweat.

The California job held so many memories for Momma. She recalled one time that Mrs. A spent $7,000 on a dress to attend a costume party, going as Mae West, the American film star. "She only wore the dress one time." This lavishness made an impression on Momma. "Can you imagine? Spending that much on one dress and never wearing it again?" she would say.

She would show us the pictures of the mansion: Mrs. A in her $7,000 dress, Patrick, her room, and the many different rooms in the house. She had lived a life that most people only dream of and that people around our town never knew existed.

The position of nanny came easily for Momma. Among the other people who worked for Mr. and Mrs. A, Momma was high in the ranks. Being the full-time caregiver for their only son was not a task taken lightly. I'm sure they saw in Momma what everyone saw—a genuine, constant, unwavering ability to care for others, and her hearing loss was not a source of concern. Her awareness of any situation was unlike most. She could feel it, see it, read it, and understand it before anyone else even knew what was happening—a perfect nanny. If she had only known at that time, even her grandchildren would call her Nanny one day.

She loved Patrick very much. I always wanted to reunite them, but Momma seemed content with just the memory. She would tell us about Mr. and Mrs. A hosting dinner parties, and her job was to make certain no one could hear Patrick, or anything for that matter, coming from their wing of the house. She said they weren't even allowed to flush toilets until all the guests had left. This was especially hard considering the goal at all other times was to teach Patrick the appropriate bathroom routine, which included flushing when finished.

She said there was one time that he flushed and thought he did good, but it was during one of their fancy parties. She sneaked to the stairs to see if any-one noticed. Fortunately, the visitors were making so much noise that "they didn't even hear the commode flush." She and Patrick just laughed. I know she was proud of the position she held and her love for Patrick was immense. I wonder if Patrick ever realized how spe-cial this nanny was, how much my future mother helped shape his life in such powerful and beautiful ways. I like to think he knew.

When she returned to Dallas, she worked full-time at the First National Bank downtown as a mail clerk. She was such a city girl. Daddy and Momma had been pen pals for the years she was away in California. How did she ever meet this country boy in the first place?

She grew up in a tiny town called Osceola near Whit-ney, Texas, and one summer day in 1965, she went with her parents to a small get-together at Uncle Bill and Aunt Pearl's house, my grandmother's brother and his family. It was an afternoon of visiting and preparing sausage. Uncle Bill had a sausage-making business, and Momma had volunteered to help, as she had many times before.

Wearing a pretty pink pressed blouse, and carrying a tray of freshly ground sausage, coming down the back steps, she glanced up to see an unfamiliar face, Daddy.

As Daddy recalls, "It was love at first sight, and I love sausage." Daddy would tell this story effortlessly with the same emphasis and word choice every time I heard it.

When their eyes first met, it probably was love at first sight for him, but Momma took things a little more seriously than most. She told us she thought he was handsome, but she didn't know anything about him. When he was about to leave, he asked her on a date. She said yes.

Momma always said that day was so pretty but a little hot. No matter what the occasion, she always made it a point to describe the weather. She had the makings to be a perfect farmer's wife, and she didn't even know it.

In the summer of 2009, she got a chance to go back to California—the second trip of a lifetime. She went with my sister, brother-in-law, and two-year-old nephew for a vacation. She flew on a plane again, which I know she had missed. She often talked about flying and how the clouds looked when you passed through them and how it felt sitting on top of them—hearing this always fascinated me. Her love for flying came through in her eyes as she would describe it.

My sister recalls the visit, remembering how happy she was to relive some of her life from a little over forty years ago. From the plane to sandy beaches to riding a ferry in San Francisco Bay to standing under a redwood tree, she got to go back where she lived a long time ago. They drove by Mr. and Mrs. A's mansion, memories flooding. The house was still gorgeous and palace-like. The smells, the sun, and everything she missed was just as it was, still there waiting for her.

In the days, weeks, and even months after the accident, I didn't watch the news or look at my weather app. I didn't give much thought to sun, rain, daytime, or nighttime. Everything was like Las Vegas casino carpet, loud and too busy to look at for very long. All my senses were on overload. Weather was no longer a concern in our family, except for one day.

We buried Momma on Saturday, August 3, 2019. Typically, this day would have carried on the grueling tradition of blinding sun and unbearable heat while covering cars and trucks with white, chalky dust. Every day of this week had been miserable, but today was the opposite. A surprise to Daddy and me, we woke up that morning to a soft, misting rain gently pushed by a cool, calming breeze. Her favorite weather. It was an early August morning that felt like a late October evening.

Daddy said, "Well, we're getting a little bit of moisture this morning." I opened the back door to put out some milk for Smoky, their cat, and felt the cooler air. It was all coming together. God was giving us Momma's favorite weather for our final goodbye. It was all meant to be for this day. Daddy and I both acknowledged the conditions outside and our morning rituals in an unusually quiet fashion. We were alone and undisturbed.

Getting ready for the service, I stood in her bathroom for what seemed like hours. I curled every piece of my hair in soft little spiral curls. I was dressed and ready to go when I went to the window to recheck the weather and noticed Daddy was outside feeding the dog. I looked at him through their small bathroom window, realizing that Momma had probably stood right there and looked at this scene many times.

It was soft outside. It was August 3, 2019, in Texas, and temperatures were in the seventies, with light rain and clouds. I knew this was a gift for her—a gift from above, a gift for us.

Around 10:00, Daddy and I left for the funeral home. Momma's service would be at 11:00, and having attended and officiated countless funerals in his lifetime, Daddy knew we should get there early for visiting in the family room. We didn't talk much that morning or on the drive. For those of you who know Daddy and me, this is quite unusual.

As I drove us down Highway 22, the delicate droplets of rain falling and splashing onto the windshield as the wipers rocked back and forth, left Daddy and me entranced in our thoughts. As I drifted further into this hypnotic state, I began to worry that the rain would cause some kind of delay or problem, but that was just my chronic case of worry-itis kicking in, always interrupting a good meditation. As I kept adjusting the wipers between low and intermittent to keep our path clear for the road ahead, the slow rain tapping on the windshield had a way of calming me back down and soothing all my fears.

As we passed the gravel road that would later take us to the cemetery where Momma would soon be, I pictured the dark green Marshall & Marshall Funeral Home tent already set up for us. I saw how it would be in just a few hours, the ones closest to her sitting with our feet on the dark green outdoor carpet, family and friends standing, but all of us grieving and still in shock.

Would it be the white chairs or the green ones? My mind started coming up with questions, such as,

How close will our chairs be to Momma?

How many seats would be available?

Who would sit by whom?

Was the tent bolted down good since it was raining and might start storming?

Which way would the procession enter the cemetery?

If they came from the side entrance, would there be enough room for all the cars?

Wait, will there be a lot of cars?

Will people come to the cemetery or just attend the funeral?

As these thoughts multiplied and raced through my head, it began to dawn on me what would be happening at that cemetery. I was good at preoccupying myself with planning and preparations. I had been doing it all week, but I suddenly stopped the questions and began to feel frightened for Momma. I remembered a story she told us about when she was a little girl, deaf and unable to speak; she couldn't make sense of death. When someone died, she didn't get the explanation that most parents give their children to calm them. She couldn't hear and hadn't started the school yet that would help her communicate. At this point, her language was all pointing, hand gestures, and facial expressions.

A close relative had passed away, and they put the body on an ironing board in the living room of their farm home. Later, when they arrived at the cemetery, she watched them lower the body and, as she explained, "in a wood box down into a big hole, so deep." This frightened Momma to her core. She couldn't believe they were doing that and she kept tugging on her mother's dress, but the only reply she received was people crossing their hands, one over the other, back and forth, in a motion to suggest no more, or all gone.

She told us she couldn't understand that, and she remained scared for quite some time. *Why did I remember this story now?* I didn't want Momma to go in the ground. I was afraid for her, and I thought maybe she wouldn't be scared if I could go in there with her. I wanted to climb in the casket so she could hold me, and I could feel her warmth again, her arms around me. I desperately wanted to be with her.

Momma was only a few hours from being put in the ground. Up until today, she was still here. I began breathing heavily, and tears filled my eyes. I knew she wasn't in her physical body anymore, but my mind continued to place her there. I hadn't mastered the separation yet. I'm not sure if I ever will.

I knew if I told anyone how I felt, they might think I'm crazy or that I need some antidepressant drug. I didn't. I needed to feel what I was feeling and embrace it. It isn't for anyone to understand, but I needed to put words to my emotions. I did. I felt it. I remember it every time I go to the cemetery. Even now, if I could get in there with her, I would, just to feel her again. I think of digging the grave up myself, not telling anyone, and putting her arms around me and mine around her.

Suddenly I came back to the drive, Daddy beside me in the passenger seat, silent. I had been doing that thing where you drive and don't really remember the speed or if you used your turn signal or how you got there. It was like I had an autonomous car, and it just knew where to take me. Daddy is usually an excellent backseat driver, and I didn't hear a peep out of him, so I assume I did okay.

Today was Momma's big day. Her last day. The day that I needed, more than anything, to be a success. I never wanted this day to come, but I never wanted it to end. Momma had always helped me plan every event, whether it was in sun, rain, ice, or snow. She was the one calm in my commotion. I didn't want to let her down. I could never repay everything she sacrificed for me, but I would give my life to make this day as perfect as she was.

As the soft and steady rain continued, approaching our destination, I saw the funeral home to my left with several cars already parked out front. As I turned on my blinker, I began to wake up from all my deep thoughts. The quiet drive had given me time to imagine the day ahead, and now it was time to be focused and strong, to do what we had all set out to do.

Feeling myself on the edge of a panic attack mixed with a few other self-diagnosed anxiety disorders, I began to hear Momma talking to me. It was so real. I remember looking at Daddy to see if he heard it, but not giving anything away if he didn't.

She was calmly saying, *Thelizabeth, just take a deep breath. Isn't this weather wonderful? Oh, I always loved this weather. Just slow down.* She had said each of those things to me before, but all at different times. At this moment, they were all back-to-back, in her voice, but we weren't facing each other or reading lips. It was only her voice whispering in my ears. Her voice was as clear as it had ever been. It was her.

Daddy went first, and some family started to come to the door to greet him and stand where I would also enter. I felt myself not wanting to go inside. I didn't want to leave the rain, Momma, her voice, or maybe I didn't want to face her last day. I'm not sure. As I slowly walked inside, I desperately hoped it would all be there when I returned—more rain, more memories, and more whispers from Momma.

When the service was over and everyone was going to their cars, our family gathered into one of the funeral home limousines. As we slowly began to pull out onto the highway, the hearse, directly in front of our car, stopped for a red light so the police could stop traffic at the intersection. I saw the rain droplets again, this time on the rear windshield of the hearse. Lying just on the other side of the wet glass was Momma, nestled in her soft, pink casket. I pictured her lying there—calm, peaceful, dry, and clean in the white satiny sheets, wearing her light pink formal dress with the tiny rectangular crystal beads on the lapel of the jacket.

She was holding in her hands a picture she had just taken a few weeks earlier of her three grandchildren—my daughter, Reagen, and my nephews, Jonah and Henry. That photo was the last time she saw them, and they saw her. Is it possible for a hearse and casket to look so beautiful?

With the rain falling so gently, it seemed as if a thin layer of peace was falling on us during this moment. I reached into the gold and crystal beaded clutch I borrowed from Momma's closet earlier that morning and pulled out my cell phone to take a picture. I didn't want to forget this scene. It was Momma's final trip home from Hillsboro, but this time there would be no last-minute run into Gap or DressBarn, no quick stop at Sonic for a Coke, and no dust to wash off the car when we got there.

The rain was God's way of showing me that Momma was okay; she was at peace. She was in a place that is always cool, breezy, with soft, misting rain, and she'll never have to feel the scalding sting of Texas summers again.

She was back in the clouds that she loved, floating above them and carrying the picture of her grandchildren with her.

Think Points

Is there a time of year that is easier or harder for you to navigate through your grief?

....
....
....
....
....
....
....
....
....
....

Is there a particular type of weather that brings you joy?

....
....
....
....
....
....
....
....
....
....
....
....
....

9

Mr. Fine

You need gentleness and support and love.
—Loretta Gale Frazier

I PAY ATTENTION TO NAMES—a doctor with the name Butcher, a dentist with the name Payne, or a carpenter with the name Wood. They often match a person's personality, may be the opposite of it, and can be funny oxymorons. Well, here in Hill County, Texas, we have Mr. Fine. This name completely matches what we all look for in a funeral director. It's all going to be fine—*Mr. Fine*, that is.

Mr. Fine carries himself with a quiet confidence, someone who seems unapproachable until you do. Dark and light tones of early gray frame his face and mouth. His eyes are a deep, soft hazel, and their intensity is vulnerable, yet subtly invasive. When he looks at you, he sees you and nothing else. He listens. He hears you. His voice is strong, yet soft. It's everything you need and want to hear, or nothing at all. All of this held hostage in a frame that walks the line daily between life and death, never knowing which side he is on.

I have found that if you say his name rather fast, it sounds like *mystified*. Mr. Fine—mystified. So much of who he is remains a mystery to me. He reminds me of Al Pacino's character in *The Godfather*, Michael Corleone. He's decisive, operates well in high-pressure situations, and commands respect—all while wearing his dark-colored suits a little oversized. He takes care of those whom he needs to and keeps his emotions in check at all times. He is silent, unless he needs to have a voice, and he is always in control. Smart and determined, but with a softness we rarely saw in Corleone. No matter who he may remind me of, he was my lifeline during both of my parents' tragic deaths. His warmth, his care, his touch. This character. This person. This man. Is Mr. Fine.

I can't emphasize enough the importance of funerals, funeral homes, and the people who work inside. The level of care and concern they give from their heart is immeasurable to what they handle from the harshest of life's happenings—death. They are there to take the body, care for the body, and in certain cases of tragic loss, they are able to create something so beautiful that you forget how your loved one ever left you.

Mr. Fine is the funeral director for a quaint, yet largely successful funeral home. Marshall & Marshall is "in our neck of the woods" as Daddy would say. This has been *the* funeral home in our area for as long as I can remember. There are two locations, one in Hillsboro and the other about fifteen minutes west of there in Whitney. Over the years, we attended many funerals, with Daddy preaching most of them, at both locations. For Momma and Daddy, the Hillsboro location is where I would see them for the last time.

I love the feeling when I'm inside this building. It's a feeling of contentment mixed with some silliness, and for just a little while, my worries are forgotten. I feel cared for. When I'm inside, my breaths are deeper, longer, slower. My anxiety begins to ease, and my racing heartbeat slows, often resulting in a yawn from exhaustion. I am more relaxed within its walls than outside them.

The atmosphere doesn't come from the building alone, it comes from the people inside. Maybe it's a feeling from everyone, or maybe it's a feeling I get from just one. The feeling of strong protection and soft comfort from a smile, a hug, a kiss on the cheek—a feeling of knowing that someone is there if you cry or if you don't. It's a rawness, a reality, a feeling of pure peace, a feeling of fullness and forever. Whatever the feeling, it is genuine, strong, and unexplained. I am still trying to put my finger on it.

It is where most of our family, a few friends from high school, all four of my grandparents, and now, where both my parents' funerals have been held. It is the last building their bodies were in. It is the last place I saw them, resting. It is the last place I was able to touch them, kiss them, smell them. It is the last building we were in together. Maybe that's why I don't mind going to the funeral home, even now, whether to pick up a copy of a death certificate, a funeral video, or maybe just to be near where they last were.

Momma

To say my mother adored Mr. Fine would be an understatement. They only saw each other on occasion, but when they did, Mr. Fine admired Momma's elegance and grace, her beauty. They had a relationship built of admiration and respect, like that of a collector of rare jewels. Momma was the cherished red ruby kept in a small, white velvet-lined box. Mr. Fine was the collector.

Over the years, I heard Momma and Daddy speak of
him, using words of love and gratitude. One day, while
sitting in the funeral home lobby waiting to take Shari
to lunch, I asked Mr. Fine, "What was it about Momma
that you loved so much?" He quickly replied, "I wanted
to hear her story." It was that simple! Mr. Fine gave
Momma the time and attention that most people do not
usually offer a deaf person. He looked at Momma completely, without reservation, and gave her the thoughtful
consideration of the one sense she was lacking—hearing.
He heard her.

Large gatherings were a constant in my parents' lives.
Funerals, weddings, church, celebrations, and no matter
what the crowd or occasion, Momma was the quiet one.
Mr. Fine went to her, sat with her, listened to her, laughed
with her, and that's what started this beautiful bond.
Above all, he listened. He wanted to hear her. He wanted
to hear how she overcame her obstacles, her difficult
childhood, and understand the everyday life of being a
deaf person, not to mention a preacher and farmer's wife.
"Sue got a double whammy," as Daddy would tell people.

Momma had talked of Mr. Fine often, but I never
paid much attention. It was part of their job, a preacher's life. I lived in another town at that time and had a
family, job, and life going on. Momma and Daddy were
always meeting different people or talking about someone that they knew from somewhere. My parents were
people-people. I just knew there was a "funeral man" that
Momma really liked.

When Momma would speak of Mr. Fine, it was

different. "The man I love at the funeral home is Mr. Fine. He is so nice." She would smile like she was talking about an old high school boyfriend. Her cheeks would blush, she would lower her chin with a shy grin, favoring Lady Diana in her early years with Prince Charles, and then finish telling us about her latest encounter with him. I was always thankful for people who recognized how extraordinary my mother was and treated her with respect, kindness, and love. For Momma, Mr. Fine was not just a name, but a familiar, friendly face that she got to know well over the past twenty years.

The week of the accident was spent planning and preparing for Momma's funeral. The most stressful time for those of us left behind is the time between when we lost them and the funeral to honor them. What an intimate relationship funeral directors have with the families during this time. I guess it's only as intimate as the family allows. There is so much to plan and figure out. Many families plan to not plan. They don't even have a funeral. Often, this is based on the wish of their loved one, but sometimes they just can't.

My heart aches when I think of all the losses and the families not able to have funerals or remembrance gatherings because of sickness or financial hardship. So many broken hearts are left to break even more because they are forced to find different ways to say goodbye. I am eternally grateful for the closeness I felt during the week of the funeral, the warmth I received from others, and the luxury of a mere touch.

When Momma's accident happened, I wasn't sure how I would go on. I couldn't bear the thought of never seeing her again. I had heard the deputy tell me what killed her. I couldn't wipe any part of what he said out of my mind. The way I remembered her was just that—a memory. I knew I would probably never see her beautiful face again. My mind was forming the pictures over and over, the images sharpening with each hour that passed, but I didn't care. I wanted to go to where she was and see her. I had images left blank to be filled in by my imagination.

Daddy said he is so glad that my sister and I didn't see her out there. Momma. Our Momma. But I would give anything to have known she was still close.

I could have held her in that space, that space in between. I could have held her in my arms. I could have felt her body again, still with some warmth of life left inside. I could have remembered a time when she was still here, still filled with life. I would have wrapped her arms around me and put my face next to hers. I would have laid with her where she was and felt her. I would take in the past with long, deep breaths, feeling the dirt going under my fingernails from the ground where I played as a child. I would bury my face in her hair, smelling the tractor's grease, covered by the scent of her purple bearded irises blooming from past springs.

I would have.

But it didn't happen that way.

That evening, as I drove up to my parents' new home just across the way from the old farmhouse, it never dawned on me that if I had turned my head to glance to my right, it's possible I would have seen some of the accident. I found out later that it had happened there and that I had only missed the first call vehicle by a few minutes. That is what they call the van or car or hearse that goes out when called to come pick up a dead body. I never thought about looking for a specific vehicle while driving closer to the farm, much less at who would be at the wheel.

Over the years I found it very impressive that when riding with Momma and Daddy in a car, no matter the occasion, they always noticed other vehicles. "There goes . . ." or "I think we just passed . . ." It's their generation. They were the generation before cell phones, satellite radio, and all the fanciness of today's automobiles. They were the generation that looks out the window instead of down at a small one. It was the generation that valued relationships with the same regard as raising their children. If Momma or Daddy had been driving to an accident involving one of us, you can bet they would have been able to give the color, make, and model on each car they passed along their way and who was driving it.

I was eagerly curious about every part of what happened in those first few minutes and hours after the accident. I didn't know what, who, when, or where exactly. I needed to know everything. I like to know exactly what happened so I can face it, accept it, and try to move past it. It took *years* to piece different portions of the events together.

Early the morning after the accident, Daddy said, "Last night they asked me where to take Sue, and I said, 'Marshall & Marshall.'" When Daddy said he directed them to take Momma to Marshall & Marshall, I called and Joni answered. She told me that Mr. Fine had brought Momma there last night. When I told Daddy this, he burst into tears. "Mr. Fine, oh, Sue would have been so glad that he got her. She loved Mr. Fine so much. We love Mr. Fine."

So Mr. Fine was driving that vehicle. He carefully and quietly picked her up out of that farm field. He did. Amid all the chaos, Mr. Fine had Momma. He drove her down that dusty gravel road, her last time to leave the farm. He drove her away. *Did he sing to her?* It dawned on me that now Momma could hear. *Did he play any music for her on their ride together?* Momma, who drove me to piano lessons for thirteen years, never hearing a note, could now hear!

I remember hearing Mr. Fine sing a duet with my sister at my Aunt Ruby Nell's graveside service in 2012. He had a powerful, yet soothing, voice. I can't remember the song, but I remember being impressed. My sister has always had a beautiful singing voice, but I had no idea Mr. Fine was also a singer. For some reason, this scene replayed when I pictured him going out there to get Momma the evening before. Momma could never quite hear the melody or make sense of music. Melody and pitch couldn't be measured, so it all just came through as noise to her, "a loud rumbling sound," as she would try to explain it to us. Now she could hear it all. Every note.

Isn't it odd how we think we know someone until we are put in their direct path, and then we see them for the first time? Their role starts to play out in our life, and we really see them. I was starting to see Mr. Fine as a person and not just a figure at the funeral home. As I attempted to put myself in his shoes, I found my awareness of him begin to evolve. I began to think of him as a friend.

What you may find as you go down this road called grief is that you will not only feel your pain but also take on the pain of others. I hurt when others hurt. The deepest parts of my heart hurt when I thought of the hot, dusty, dirty, and grotesque scene he arrived to find that late July day. Their last scene together, the scene where he picks her up and carries her away.

As I learned a few more details about how that all went down, so to speak, I found out Mr. Fine went to get Momma by himself. I can't imagine that. I know this is his profession, but it's not a job to be taken lightly. He knew Momma. He really knew her. How hard that must have been.

I wanted to return some comfort to Mr. Fine for the hurt and sadness he had to endure just because that was his job. All I kept thinking about was writing him a thank-you card, but instead it turned into a chapter. He gets a chapter in this book. And it's still not enough.

Over Daddy's tears, sobs, and cries, I tried to listen to what Joni was saying. She said there was a matter they needed to ask me about. I said, "Yes, what is it?" She asked if I gave permission for Momma to be embalmed. She said they are required to ask and get approval for this to be done.

In all my years being exposed to death through Daddy's ministry and funeral services, I never knew that they had to ask permission. I just thought it happened. It was a shock to me, but I knew what it meant. So I immediately acted accordingly (as if I knew the routine) and said, "Yes, of course." When hanging up the phone, I debated telling this part of our conversation to Daddy. Keeping in mind Daddy's meticulous attention to detail, I told him. He said firmly, "Yes, we have to do that."

There was normalcy in the planning and preparation for Momma's big day, her funeral. I knew, in that moment, that Daddy needed this funeral as much as or more than anyone. We all did.

As the week progressed, plans started coming together. The funeral service is similar to a wedding, but instead of a year to plan, you get a week, sometimes two. You cram that year of planning into those few days, add the stress and sadness, and what you're left with is pain—headaches, stomachaches, body aches, and sleeplessness. Yep! You have grief. That's the diagnosis.

Daddy

Daddy was a storyteller and a historian, and nostalgia should have been his middle name. Joe *Nostalgia* Boyd, not Joe Bob Boyd. If Daddy had a captive audience of one, he had an audience.

Mr. Fine is a lover of history and loved hearing his stories. This should be all I write about their relationship because that's all either of them needed. They made a perfect pair, one who told stories and the other who listened to those stories. This fact alone gave me a good understanding of their relationship.

After Momma's accident, their friendship graduated to a new, more personal level. They had a quiet, intimate understanding of each other, their sadness, their memory of that day, and their deep respect for each other's role in it.

After I found Daddy that Father's Day morning, I was soon surrounded by friends, family, and emergency responders. As I walked back and forth on the driveway and through my parents' front yard, I was silently searching for him—Mr. Fine. Shari was there. Joni was there. Levin, another friend from the funeral home, had brought the van that would take Daddy away from the farm this last time. All these people had become more than friends; they were family, yet through my haze and shock, I continued glancing down the driveway to see what car was coming next.

Where was he? Where was Mr. Fine?

Shari had been working for Marshall & Marshall Funeral Home for over a year now, and I saw this as an added bonus, considering she wasn't working there when Momma had died. I frantically asked her and Joni to call. "Call Mr. Fine. Can you call Mr. Fine?"

I was asking like a child wanting to go play at a friend's house, with my hands pushed together in front of me, as if I was about to pray. I was anxiously wanting to see and be surrounded by him, be cared for by him. The feeling I get from him is as subtle as laying a soft blanket on a baby and as strong as pulling a trailer of Brahma bulls up a steep, rocky road.

I knew I needed him. And maybe because of his respect and love for my parents, he needed me too.

Joni let me know she had just spoken to him, but he was out of town. A wave of relief washed over me. I had lost so many things recently, and I didn't want to lose that connection—the connection that drew me in like a lighthouse that shines for a lost ship. I needed the comfort that I had felt the last time a tragedy had taken one of my parents, a comfort that he provides. I often think I should have a note safety-pinned to my shirt, like in elementary school, that says, "In case of death, please take me to Mr. Fine." I will never take for granted the caring and kindness the funeral people give every day to everyone. It's a feeling like no matter what, it's going to be okay.

It's going to be *fine*. Mr. Fine.

His name is James.

Think Points

Is there someone you feel understands your grief more than others?

....
....
....
....
....
....
....
....

How have they helped you?

....
....
....
....
....
....
....
....

Write them a short thank-you note here:

....
....
....
....
....
....
....

10

The Final Goodbyes

Hearts may break and shatter, but love remains.
—Theo Boyd

Momma

I believe a casket says a lot about a person. There are several ways to decide how your body will be *handled* when you die. Many people are deciding to be cremated rather than buried. For the Boyd family, we are the traditional, casket-buried-in-the-ground people.

As Mr. Fine led us around that room, showing us different options, my breathing was becoming tighter, faster, more uncontrolled. The casket room can do that to a person. It was like walking through RoomStore or Haverty's furniture store, but instead of couches and coffee tables, it was caskets in all different finishes and colors. It can be overwhelming because the reality is literally lying in front of you. Daddy didn't go in this room with us. He said that he wanted us to pick it out. "You girls know what Sue likes."

As we looked around, my sister and I were in agreement that Momma didn't like "too busy" or "too much." She was simple. She was elegant. She was that rare jewel who only needed a soft box to hold her. *She* was enough. Mr. Fine knew this. He knew her style.

After a few minutes, we couldn't find what we were looking for, if we even knew what that was. It felt like we were in some type of eerie gameshow where you are given just so many minutes to buy something you will have to live inside forever.

Mr. Fine could sense our uneasiness. He left for a moment and then came back with a catalog in hand. Once again, I felt as if I were picking out a new piece of furniture for my living room. I wish that was all it was.

We looked, flipping the pages rapidly, beginning to panic that we wouldn't find what we wanted. Then, there it was. We both said, "This one!" Mr. Fine looked and said, "Well, that one is actually on clearance." We started laughing. "It's meant to be. Momma loved a good sale!" He chuckled. We had no idea about pricing, nor did it matter, but how appropriate that even in her death she was getting a good deal. She would have loved that. We selected a pale pink casket for Momma, and it was beautiful. Just beautiful. Mr. Fine agreed, "It's her."

My breathing began to return to normal, and we were able to go back to Daddy and tell him how perfect the casket was. It was like when we were little, picking wildflowers, holding them in our sweaty hands and eagerly taking them to Momma, who would then show Daddy what a pretty bouquet she got. It was as if she were with us, even in the casket room, guiding us to pick the perfect one.

For Momma, it would be a closed casket service. There was really no decision to be made. Momma had suffered a severe head injury. I could only imagine what Daddy saw and felt when he jumped off that tractor, knowing what had just happened. Momma was right there. She was reaching up, and Daddy was reaching down. He leaned to his right, and his left leg lifted off the clutch. Momma was right in front of that big tractor tire, and then gone. In the blink of an eye, in one instant, the way I saw the world changed forever. I was now looking at a world without a mother. She was gone, and I was alone.

About two days after Momma's accident, while at the funeral home making arrangements, I had questions. I still wanted to see her. My desire to be near her had intensified. Not wanting Daddy to hear the conversation, my sister and I stepped into the hallway. Mr. Fine was leading the way. He let us know that there was a tremendous amount of swelling and that every bone in her head, face, and neck had been broken and completely crushed. Understanding our curiosity, he used his hands to show what path the tire had crossed over her body. It had passed over her upper torso from the left lower part of her shoulder up to the right and everything in between. Her arms, hands, and everything below her shoulders were undamaged. Since there was such significant injury to the part of Momma we wanted to see the most, her face, Mr. Fine was not sure of what the preparations and the result was going to look like.

"It's going to be tough," he said with slight hesitation, as he cleared his throat, taking a slightly deeper breath than I had heard from him before.

As he slowly walked back toward the room where Daddy was, he whispered, "I don't think she ever knew."

This was comforting and disturbing all at the same time. When tragedy strikes, we want to know that our loved one didn't suffer. We want answers. We need them, and if we don't get answers, it prolongs our agony and deepens our pain, our hurt, our grief.

As we made our way back to Daddy, I found myself wanting to know more. I was happy with what he did share, but until I could see her with my own eyes, I couldn't believe she was really gone. Whether she looked like Momma or not, I didn't care. I needed to see, smell, and touch her. Mr. Fine knew this.

I made a quick call to Momma's hairdresser, Reyna, at All About Hair. This was the little beauty shop in downtown Hillsboro that Momma and Daddy visited regularly.

"We love Reyna," Momma would say. I asked Reyna if she would be able to go to the funeral home and do Momma's hair. I explained the situation with regard to the damage to Momma. I didn't want her to say she could when maybe she couldn't. This would be hard for her, for anyone. She said, "Yes, I can." There was no hesitation in her voice. She loved Momma and wanted to do this for her. She was a strong woman who had lived through many difficult times in her life, which is why the bond she had with my parents was so strong. They listened to one another through the years—talking, sharing, joking, and caring for one another. Who doesn't love their hairdresser, right?

I wanted Momma to be beautiful for Momma. She always took such great care of herself and had a purposeful amount of pride in her appearance. She was always "fixed up." I needed her to be herself—forever beautiful.

"She still had rollers in her hair," Mr. Fine whispered in a gentle tone.

"Yes, she had just taken a shower. She rolled her hair. We thought she was in for the day, but she wasn't. She wasn't." I blurted all this out, as if I had found a missing piece to a secret puzzle. Mr. Fine saw what we had forgotten—the rollers.

"Did she have her hearing aid on?" I continued to search for more pieces.

"Yes, she did," he replied.

"Can you please take it off? Momma never wanted to be buried with her hearing aid because she said she wouldn't need it anymore."

"I can try," he replied with hesitation.

We left this alone. We had to prioritize what was most important, and we knew she was in Heaven, no hearing aid needed. If he didn't think this was possible, then we trusted him in that decision.

Sensing the shock and sadness that my sister and I were feeling in this moment, Mr. Fine began to tell us something that brought such warmth to our cold reality.

He told us that a baby died on the same day as our momma. The baby was there at the funeral home. He explained how he moved the table with the baby over to be close to Momma's table and left them there each night together, Momma with the precious little baby next to her.

"Last night, I told Sue to 'take care of that baby now,'" repeating what he said to Momma.

All I could think of in this moment was how lucky this baby was to have Momma with him. He wasn't there alone. Part of me felt jealous of this baby. He had the best and most cherished mother, my mother, with him, and she had him. She wasn't here with me anymore. She was with him. I was alone, but they weren't. They had each other. As I began to realize the beauty of this, my jealousy faded. I was so thankful and felt it an honor to hear the most intimate details of what was such a raw and rare moment.

Later that afternoon, I picked up the local newspaper, *The Reporter*, to see Momma's obituary in black and white. There it was. And right beside it was the photo of a baby. I saw the face of that precious baby, and he was lying right beside her on the page in front of my very tearful eyes. I could now visualize exactly what Mr. Fine had explained. That baby. My momma. They had each other.

The next day, Thursday, August 1, 2019, my daddy, my sister, and I got to see Momma. We got a call early Thursday morning from Joni that Momma should be ready by 6:00 that evening. I was comforted to know I would soon see her again.

When we arrived, Mr. Fine greeted us. He gave me a hug and a soft kiss on the temple. I immediately felt understood. No words had to be spoken. How we felt, how he felt, how we all felt was delivered in the way that Momma understood best—body language.

I pulled Momma's glasses from my purse, handing them over to Joni. She had been waiting on them and said it would help. She went into the room, the room Momma was in, and told us to wait for a minute. Mr. Fine went over and started talking to Daddy about weather or farming, to keep him occupied and possibly comfort him, while my sister and I prepared to see Momma for the last time. We didn't know what to expect, but we knew it would be Momma.

Joni came back and asked us not to touch Momma's face. She wanted to make sure we knew this and gave special attention by pointing to her own forehead, nose, and cheeks. It didn't matter what we saw; it was Momma, and we just wanted to be with her.

As we walked in the big, open room, we glanced to the left. There was the clearance casket we had picked out the day before, and Momma was lying inside. She was peaceful. She looked so pretty and pink. We couldn't believe it. Much to our surprise, we were not overcome with sadness; we were relieved. About that time, Mr. Fine came in. We hugged him. He seemed tired, completely worn out, emotionally and physically spent. We told him how much she looked like Momma. We didn't know how to thank him. We couldn't quit saying it. "Thank you so much. She's beautiful."

Daddy came in. We held him. He cried, but mostly I believe he was in shock. We all were. I even think Mr. Fine may have been. Sure, this was his job, and he had done this for years, but it was different. So different.

After Daddy got seated in the room, my sister and I sat. We all just sat with our thoughts, in the quiet. We sat with our memories of her. We sat with our memories of her with us. We were in the room with her. Just in the room. Being present with her like she had always been with us.

We debated for a few minutes about having an open casket. After we talked, we realized Momma never really liked to think of herself in the casket with people looking at her. She would often comment and say, "I hope I'm not in an open casket. I don't want people looking at me." Joni also mentioned that in cases such as this, often human nature tends to cause people to gawk or stare, as their curiosity about "what really happened" gets the better of them.

Daddy, my sister, and I all decided right then that Momma always wanted a closed casket anyway. So, closed it would be. This suited her. Knowing how beautiful she was inside that delicate pink casket helped all of us feel at peace with the decision.

Later we learned that it had taken approximately thirteen hours of work to prepare Momma for us. No wonder Mr. Fine seemed worn out. I can't and won't ever be able to thank him enough for what he gave us.

Mr. Fine gave us our final goodbye. This moment was the last time I smelled her hair, touched her skin, lightly brushed my lips over her face, and whispered, "I love you, Momma" in her ear, knowing she could hear me this time. Mr. Fine did this for me. He did this for us.

Daddy

For Daddy, it would be the same, but opposite all at the same time.

I picked out a light gray suit with hints of soft purple thread woven throughout, a lavender shirt, still hanging in its dry cleaner's bag, with a coordinating silver, navy, and lavender tie that I had given him for Father's Day a few years before. It was so pretty how it all blended together perfectly. I loved picking out ties for Daddy. I always had. He had so many. It seemed that every holiday or birthday, I would get Daddy a tie with a matching dress shirt.

As I ran the back of my hand across the ties in his closet, my mind replayed scenes of when I had given him a certain tie or what comment Momma had made about it. "That's so pretty." "I like that." "That looks so good, Joe." I could hear her voice.

I took longer than usual to pick out his last dress suit and tie, but is there a time limit on picking out final clothes? I buried my nose into his clothes hanging there, smelling Daddy in that closet once again. I buried my face in all of it. I longed to smell the man I ran to, who would pick me up, twirl me around, and put me on his shoulders. I craved the smell of a memory from our daddy-daughter dance.

With Momma, I had tried to smell her, but she kept herself and everything so clean that we couldn't catch a hint. With Daddy, there was some sand mixed with a little dirt and grease, but his suits were kept nice and clean.

Daddy would get a boutonniere to wear before services. It was only fitting that he wore one. He was usually the preacher at these things and would get one anyway.

With the suit, the boutonniere, and making sure that Daddy was as nicely prepared as our Momma had been, we knew his would also be a closed casket. Daddy had also died tragically. We knew he had suffered a gunshot to the head. We didn't expect that Daddy could have an open casket, as he had always liked through the years. "I wish they would have an open casket. People need to see the body." Daddy was traditional to a fault. He liked to be able to see the body and tell it goodbye.

With Daddy, we made arrangements on a Wednesday, the same as Momma. The arrangements went smoothly. We picked out a beautiful wood casket from the casket room. It was solid wood, reminding us of a tree that Daddy had written a poem about. This poem was going to be in his funeral program.

A Boy's First Long Journey

Last summer of 2011, an old, very familiar Oak tree died.
I must tell you though, I am now sixty-eight,
and my memories of this old tree will never die.

This tree, along with three other old oak trees,
has always stood over in the pasture, halfway between
Mother and Daddy's house and Grandma and
Grandpa Boyd's old house.

When I was just a four- or five-year-old boy,
I took one of my first longest journeys of about
one-quarter mile over to Grandma's house.
Under this particular oak tree,
I would always stop and decide
whether I should continue on or go back home to Mother.

What a big world everything seemed
to be back then to a little boy.

As I now stand as a tired and retired adult
under this old dead oak tree,
my mind and heart reflect back to those days
of my boyhood.

I seem to recall a line from a poet
and his poem of years gone by.
He said, "I think I shall never see anything
as lovely as a tree."
And I must say, "To that, I agree."

—Joe Bob Boyd

Mr. Fine helped us once again, guiding us through the casket room. I was having a hard time holding it together. It was different this time. I didn't have to stay strong for Daddy sitting back in the other room. I didn't have to hide my emotions from anyone. There was no one whom I had to pretend I was okay for anymore.

I was grieving Momma again, or maybe for the first time.

Mr. Fine put his hand on my back. He led me around the room, and another funeral person came in to help lighten the mood. Chuck was good at keeping things funny. I collected myself. After all, this funeral had to be "the funeral of all funerals," as I kept telling everyone. Daddy deserved the best because he did so much for everyone else's funerals all through the years. Momma would have wanted it to be a final thank-you from everyone that he had ever preached a funeral for, a thank-you for all the years he gave of himself to others.

When in the room, making arrangements, I couldn't believe that my last parent was also going to have a closed casket funeral. I had seen Daddy after I found him that Sunday morning. I remembered, too vividly, what I saw.

"Closed casket," my sister and I said simultaneously. Mr. Fine lowered his head, cleared his throat, looked out of the top of his glasses, and said, "Why don't you wait to see him before you decide." I was surprised. *Would it be possible that Daddy could have what he had always wanted, an open casket?*

That afternoon, I gathered a few more things from the house—his worn and weathered work boots, his shoeshine box, and his perfectly kept dark blue FFA (Future

Farmers of America) corduroy jacket from high school. I
also reached for a frame with a 5x7 black-and-white photo
of Momma. It was Daddy's favorite picture of her. It was
taken when they had gotten engaged in August 1969. She
looked radiant and poised. He had it on his desk for as
long as I could remember, and now I was disturbing it. I
took it out of the frame, opening the back for the first time
since it had been placed inside. I gently pulled it away
from the glass, and it was perfect.

We had buried Momma holding a picture of their
three grandchildren in her hands, but Daddy would hold
a picture of Momma. This picture. His favorite picture
of her.

I made another trip into Hillsboro to deliver the items
I had gathered. I kept the picture to myself. I was too
afraid something could happen to it. I kept it in between
two tissues lying in the passenger seat next to me. When I
got home, I put it in a manila folder that I had and placed
it by the back door.

The next day, Shari called and said Daddy was there
and ready. It was Thursday morning. Daddy had been
there for less than twenty-four hours, coming in from
another town where he had been sent for an autopsy when
he left the farm. I learned this was standard protocol when
a death was unattended and involved a gunshot wound.

My sister and I got there as quickly as we could. We
walked in. Joni and Shari were there. Shari showed us
into the room where Daddy was lying. It wasn't the same
room that Momma had been in, but it was right across
the hall. And there he was. Daddy. With his lavender

shirt, gray suit, and boutonniere, he was as handsome as he always was.

He was at peace. He was resting. He looked as if he were about to stand and preach a service. He looked like our daddy. With just me and my sister there, we took turns being with him. My sister said she was trying to think of a word to describe how he looked. She had a word in mind, but it was taking her a while to process.

I was speechless. I had remembered what I saw just three days before, but those images were slowly being erased as I stood there looking at him. I held the photo that I had brought from the frame on his desk.

"Daddy, here is that picture of Momma you love." My tears began to fall. I noticed they were leaving tiny wet circles on his suit. At first, I was upset that I may be messing up his suit, but the drops vanished quickly. The pattern of falling and fading teardrops continued as I stood beside him, over him. They became a slow and steady rain.

"Dignified." My sister finally thought of the word.

Daddy lay there in that beautiful wooden casket. Dignified.

Not being given any instructions or warnings as we had with Momma, I took full advantage. I laid my head and arms over his body. I smelled his suit, just like I had smelled it in the closet the day before. I touched his hands, just like I had touched them the morning I found him. They were colder now. I made my way to his face, smelling what I pretended was Old Spice or Campho-Phenique, but it wasn't. It was a smell I have a hard time explaining. It smelled like emptiness and fullness, like his old closet inside a new mansion. He wasn't there, but I could pretend in that moment that he was.

I told him how much I loved him and how it was all okay. "It's okay, Daddy. It's okay." "I love you so much, Daddy." "Please don't be gone, but it's okay." "It's okay." I repeated the same words I said when I found him. Just repeated them all.

Reality hit me as hard as I could imagine the bullet hit him. Sharp, instant, forced. It was a reality that I still have difficulty grasping. It was life and death and everything in between all at once. It was awful, beautiful, miserable, comforting, sour, and sweet. Bittersweet, they call it. It was all bittersweet.

Months later, I would receive the autopsy report. I read it word for word, looking for the specifics of everything. I was searching for answers that no one would know, especially a medical examiner. I read about the trajectory of the bullet, the entrance point, the weight of each of his organs, and yet in all of this, I was still hoping to know more. With suicide, that is just how it will always be. We may never know exactly what took them to that moment, the moment they pulled the trigger.

With Daddy, at least we knew why. Daddy left the farm the way he wanted to. Daddy knew that he would be with Momma. He couldn't take the pain of her death any longer, and he was ready for his final goodbye.

Think Points

☐ Do you know how you want your body to be handled after death? Cremated, buried, donated to science?

....
....
....
....
....
....
....
....
....

☐ Have you notified people close to you of your wishes?

....
....
....
....
....
....
....
....
....
....
....
....

11

More "F" Words

With a friend, life has no end.
—Theo Boyd

Fabulous, Faithful, Forever . . .

Friends!

Friends!

Friends!

There are people who God will put in your path, and until events of this magnitude happen, you have no idea how important their role will be in your now-shattered life. These lifesavers play a very important part in helping you, loving you, and giving you the support you need to make it through the worst time of your life. They help you to get better and be better.

The network of friends I have runs many miles long, and once connected, watch out. These ladies could rule the world. With one phone call you can set in motion a bond of females who'll act as the Salvation Army, United Way, the Red Cross, Army, Navy, Air Force, and Marines all at the same time. The strength in this web of women could win any Ironwoman competition, leaving the others not just beaten, but blown away.

If you have ever watched the popular television show from the 1980s called *Designing Women*, then you already know three of my closest friends. Funny, eccentric, unique, and if there ever needed to be a reality show, they are it. They are decorators and owners of the cutest little clothing store in the town where I lived before moving back to my hometown.

Charlene, Charlotte, and Michele—Flamboyant, Fabulous, Faithful, Fearless, and Forever there for me. Their shop is called The Mix, and that's a perfect description of these three—a mix of all the best "F" words. What some people don't know is that two of these ladies also own funeral homes and a flower shop. Yes, they know death all too well. They know death so well they're able to find the humor in any situation. There is no doubt that God brought us together because he knew how much I would need them in my life. Isn't it awesome when we see God working in real time and don't have to wait for it? Sent to rescue me from life's blows, they always appear when I've been knocked down to help me surface again. They are there. Holding me. I call them my fairy blonde-mothers.

Momma

In 2019, during the week of Momma's funeral preparations, something phenomenal happened. The flowers came pouring into the funeral home. I was online reviewing the arrangements to make sure everything was error-free, and I noticed the postings on Momma's tribute wall. As I scrolled down, it didn't stop. I scrolled and scrolled and scrolled—the comments and floral orders became more than I could count. *Uh-oh! I had better contact the local flower shops to get Momma's big sprays ordered.* All the flower shops I called informed me they were out of flowers.

What? No flowers! What are we going to do?

The Mix to the rescue! With their shop being only thirty minutes down the road from the funeral home, they would "take care of all the flowers." And they did. Momma's casket spray and all her flowers were the most beautiful I have ever seen.

I won't forget them.

When my daughter was a baby, I held her in my arms, paying special attention to what her eyes looked like as we rocked in unison forward and back. Resting my left elbow on the arm of the rocker, I cradled her inside, my hands entwined under her body, and with nothing else to distract me, I memorized her. I didn't want to forget her eyes, their depth, their color, their flawless sparkle, and I didn't. Looking at me, looking at her, remembering the moment. Her eyes reached inside to my soul, awakening parts of me that had never been touched until I had her. I can still close my eyes and remember her eyes exactly— her brows, her lashes, her lids opening and closing as they looked up at me. I still see their beauty.

I smelled the top of her soft head, her full face, gently running my cheek along hers. Closing my eyes, I kissed her temple, my lips staying connected. I recorded the memory of her at the slowest speed possible. I smelled her, fully capturing the sensation that was only her. Quick, shallow breaths followed by one deep inhale, causing both of us to yawn, I would repeat this pattern until I had her deeply ingrained in my memory. My baby girl is saved in the smallest, most precious place inside. It's a place I go to right before I fall asleep, right before I pray, or when I listen to a song that takes me back to the place where I first recorded it all. This is how it is for me with Momma's funeral flowers.

When I first saw them, I was breathless. Their beauty and their shapes, their smells, all were being slowly recorded as I scanned them with each inhale. I closed my eyes, gently brushed my nose against a rose, nesting in its petals. I took in a deep, long breath to store in a place I can pull from and feel again.

With each smell, I remember the sweetness, and I remember Momma. I smell the colors, and it takes me back to everything—the accident, the funeral, the beauty of her, and the flowers. Oh, the flowers. The majestic bouquets with shades of pink, purple, and white were her final farewell, but they remain my constant reminder. Each time I smell a flower's bloom or stop to smell the roses, as they say, I remember it all. These fragrant reminders stayed with her, lying on top of her grave, covering her each night like a blanket keeping her warm.

At the time of Momma's death, I had only just begun a friendship with the ladies at The Mix. During the past three years, that friendship has grown in the most natural way possible. We all just love being with one another. They were there for me in times of sadness, gladness, and all the while, they had cute clothes in their shop for any occasion. They are blessings in so many ways.

When my marriage began falling apart, they were there. When my days and nights were lonely, they were there. I had been talking to them daily for months, and then, on Father's Day 2022, I would be needing them once again in many ways. Déjà vu had become a never-ending theme in my life.

I was like a red ant bed when life kicked me. Everything seemed scattered and ruined, but the troops just got a new mission. They began working to move me forward, using one another's strengths to protect, preserve, and purposefully build up a new fort of protection around me.

Daddy

After I found Daddy and made the emergency call to 911 and called my sister, I dialed several other numbers. I called my friends. Having many levels and categories of friends in my network, I knew which ones could ignite the chain reaction I knew I would need. It was a "mix" of friends and family that I held in my palm and in my heart.

"You just can't make this shit up, Theo!" Charlotte blurted out as she stepped out of her car. Immediately, she had the attention and love of those of us standing outside. Everyone in that setting, that moment, knew the contagion of events life had handed me over the past three years. We all needed to laugh a little. What a welcome relief from the sweetest of friends.

These ladies would, once again, be my emergency florist and decorators. They really outdid themselves for Daddy's funeral. They began planning from the moment they stepped in the house and into their new roles for the week, Theo's personal assistants for all things funeral. They took a few framed prints off the hallway walls, and I didn't question them. I knew they were going to do something pretty spectacular. Boy, did they!

What can you say about friends who will stuff over four hundred small burlap bags with peanuts for your Daddy's visitation and funeral? Goodie bags! I had never thought of goodie bags at a funeral, but people loved this. These fairy blonde-mothers took a framed column I had written from several years ago, "Proud to Be a Peanut Farmer's Daughter," and placed it inside a beautiful spray of sunflowers, peanuts, and daisies, all beautifully wrapped with a burlap sash. They took Daddy's FFA jacket and displayed it with Daddy's boots, shoeshine kit, and high school yearbooks in a most beautiful display along the wall where the casket lay.

As you entered the funeral home, in the foyer, everything was decorated in the way only The Mix can do. Momma's favorite picture of Daddy that she had taken over ten years before greeted people as they came through the front doors. I ordered this canvas in a 40x50 black-and-white. This photo was of Daddy's profile, and it told a story of a farmer, his hard work, and captured the essence of who he was.

Flowers were placed in perfect position, allowing people to walk and see Daddy's life with each step into the sanctuary. My youngest nephew and I purchased some watermelons and cantaloupes to put in bushel baskets around the casket. While we were in the grocery store, our cart full, people were asking my nephew about the party we must be getting ready for. "These are for the baskets at my Bob's funeral." His innocent answer took me back as the reality of what we were doing hit me like a tsunami—rushing by, flooding my senses with the memories of being out in the field with Daddy.

The spray of flowers on top of Daddy's casket were as beautiful as Momma's had been. They showed Daddy's love of Texas wildflowers and sun, bold colors that caught the eye, complementing the wood they lay on with sprinkles of peanuts throughout. Daddy always loved flowers. He would say, "At my funeral I want flowers. I love them. Make donations on your own time, but I would just love flowers." His flowers and funeral were one of the most beautiful I have ever seen. It was a memorable tribute to a Texas farmer and my daddy.

In learning to live with my losses, as traumatic as they have been, I had friends who were my anchors, helping me to stay on the path to become me again. Although I believe at times they worried.

"Oh, Theo, one can only handle so much."

"Geez, Theo, if I were you, I wouldn't be able to get out of bed."

"Oh, girl, God has a plan for you so much bigger than what you can see right now."

It was through these friends, their words, their actions, and their love, that I am able to finish this book and bring it to you. Do you have friends like these? If you have just one, lean on them. It doesn't have to be a big network. Remember, I like to talk, and I am a people-person, so it comes easily for me. If you are more reserved, it's okay.

Step out and lean! Learning to live through this thing called grief takes more than yourself.

Sure, God can be and should be all we need, but God gave us people to fellowship with, so do that. Let the friends come and do what they do best. I believe God gives us hope through our friendships. Hope is found when our friends find us in our time of need.

Here are a few more examples of my friends and how they helped me. I wanted to mention every single person I encountered on this journey who has helped me, but that wouldn't fit in this book. So, maybe I'll write another one.

Dina—She would ignite all the moms I had come to know throughout the years. Our daughters grew up together, went to school together, and we shared some funny memories of the same obstetrician who had delivered them. Dina knew which people to contact, but she also knew my momma and daddy well. Having lost both her parents, she and I would often comment on how my parents had adopted her as their own. Our daughters spent weeks in the summer with Momma and Daddy and have stayed close even into their young adulthood. Dina would be multitasking during this week. She would continue to be a second mother to my daughter, a party planner for helping with the small family lunch after the funeral, and she would step in to do anything that would arise during the week and for weeks after. She drove down immediately and met me in Daddy's yard within the hour after I had called her, and it was the same when Momma died. That's just my Dina.

Amberly—She would ignite the teacher network. We taught high school together, and our bond was strong enough to command 150 sixteen-year-olds, all the while making plans for dinner and exchanging girl talk when leaving campus to grab a quick iced tea. She and her husband have six children, so my respect for her is immense. She also helped me with my family-leave plan and getting a full-time substitute when Momma died. Here we were again, but I didn't need the family leave—I just needed her. I needed my teachers around me in thoughts and prayers. I needed to see their sweet faces to remind me of the happier times and the love we shared in seeing hope in the young eyes we taught.

Allison—For this sweet friend, it was a voice mail that I listened to over and over. She is more than a friend; she was like a sister. We grew up seeing each other only in the summers, riding my go-cart, swimming in little plastic pools, and playing together for as long as our parents would allow. She lived in New York, but her grandmother lived only a short walk away from our farm so they would come visit Texas in the summers. Allison's mom and my daddy went on their very first date together. Our families were a part of one another's lives, and she was still a part of mine. She would call me each day to check on me when Momma died and to cry with me when Daddy died. She is still a constant confidant and treasure.

And then there is **Lea** . . .

For her, it would be a text. Just like with Momma, I could not speak on the phone with Lea. We have a great friendship that we maintain over text. She was so much like my mother in her hearing loss, both having such similar stories. Having her in my life has been a blessing of reminders on how strong a woman can be when she is faced with a loss such as this, her hearing. I met her when I started teaching high school. She was the American Sign Language teacher, and we bonded immediately. When she speaks, I hear the unique voice that was only my mother's.

For several weeks after Momma died and I had returned to teaching, I couldn't be around Lea. I wanted to, but her voice reminded me so much of Momma that it stirred up emotions I just couldn't handle while teaching. Then one day, I decided to go to her classroom. I walked down the hallway and all the way to her classroom at the other end of our school building. I peeked through her window, and she saw me and quickly signed to the class to give her a minute. She came outside her classroom door, and I hugged her so tightly. I wrapped my arms around her as if I was hugging Momma again. Her voice, our love for each other, and the special bond we share was made stronger that day.

Karla and **Brittany**—They would ignite the friends from my old days in the banking and business communities. They were also there for me during my most recent heartbreak and the marriage that fell apart. Karla knew the people that other friends wouldn't have known. She lived in Arkansas now, but she was with me by texting, calling, and praying for me. From the moment we met, we knew we were long-lost sisters. We bonded and never stopped. Although I don't get to see her often, the times when we do, we never miss a beat, laughing, crying, and loving each other.

Brittany would contact her mom, Lisa, who spent countless hours on the phone with Daddy over the past three years, listening, singing, and just helping him pass the time in his "just existing" life. Lisa showed up at the house the morning that Daddy left us. Brittany had made the call to her mom to "go see Theo now," and she came to spend the day, working as if she were a hired hand on the farm. Her love was oozing out through her acts of kindness for me and my sister, attending to our every need. She was such a comfort that day and every day since. Brittany would surprise me the next day.

I am at Daddy's house, struggling. I am sitting at his desk trying my best to write the perfect obituary to get things ready for the funeral. I hear Daddy's dog, Barney, barking, I open the door to the garage, and there she is. Déjà vu setting in once again. It was just like when Momma had passed. Summer, hot, dry, and sad. We didn't exchange words. We just stood and hugged each other for what seemed like an hour.

When Momma died, Brittany had walked the same path, through the garage, and we met in the doorway. No words. She was there, hugging us, hugging Daddy, letting him sob and cry. No words needed.

This time, she would come in and sit for hours on the floor of Daddy's bedroom, sorting through countless photos for the slide show that would be playing at the visitation and funeral. It was during this quiet time that I was able to write the obituary for Daddy, and it was perfect.

Joe Bob Boyd

December 19, 1943 ~ June 19, 2022

Joe Bob Boyd passed away at his home in Whitney on Sunday, June 19, 2022, at the age of 78. Funeral services will be held at 11:00 a.m. Saturday, June 25, 2022, at Marshall & Marshall Funeral Directors Chapel in Hillsboro with Pastor David Gant and Rev. Roy Frink officiating. Burial will follow at Peoria Cemetery. Visitation will be held from 6:00-8:00 p.m. Friday, June 24, at the funeral home.

Joe Bob was born to Steve "Henry" and Lilly Elizabeth (Roberts) Boyd, December 19, 1943, in Whitney, Texas. As a young boy, he loved going out in the woods with his friends, fishing for crawdads, hunting squirrels, eating frog legs, and swimming in tanks. He loved camping out and would often stay "gone too long" as his mother would say. Joe Bob loved dirt. He loved the land, and being a farmer and rancher was as thick in his blood as the sand in his boots. Peanuts, watermelons, cantaloupe, black-eyed peas, and hogs, pigs, cattle, chickens, a dog named "Doodle-um" and a horse named "Paint."

His mother's prayer was that Joe Bob would one day become a preacher. At the age of nine, he accepted the Lord as His personal Savior, but it didn't stop there. Joe Bob began to live for the Lord in a way that put most of us to shame. He taught Sunday School, Vacation Bible School, led the song service, and even sat in some of the "longest revival meetings in Texas." He was later ordained a pastor and was told by the scholars at Dallas Theological Seminary that he was the most knowledgeable self-taught individual they had ever encountered. On a corner of his father's land—he had a vision to build a church. It was there that he led Bethel Bible Church for 33 years, supporting missionaries around the world, and assisting anyone in the community that needed him.

Joe Bob married Sue Worlow on January 10, 1970, and together they were a witness to their community and beyond for 50 years. Joe Bob was the farmer, rancher, and preacher while Sue was his helpmate in all of those things and more. You rarely saw one without the other. Joe Bob was the funny one in an International Tractor cap and denim work shirt, while Sue was the quiet one wearing a silk blouse and heels.

Preceding him in death were his wife, Sue Worlow Boyd, his parents, Steve "Henry" and Lille Elizabeth Boyd, two sisters, Ruby Nell Boyd and Bessie Marie Curry, and one brother, Steve Boyd, Jr.

Survivors include his two daughters, Thelizabeth Boyd, Hannah Jo Boyd and husband, Ronald; and three grandchildren, Reagen Thomas, Jonah Locke, and Henry Hehmann, along with numerous nieces, nephews, and cousins.

"And we know that all things work together for good to them that love God, to them who are the called according to his purpose."
—Romans 8:28

Joe Bob Boyd, 1969

David (my high school friend)—David would ignite my old high school "Class of 1990" from Whitney. David had been a part of Daddy and Momma's life for so many years. He was a pallbearer at both funerals. He formed a bond with them back in our old high school days. Hunting deer on their land, taking them fishing, and spending countless hours with them over the years, especially the last few, David and my parents had a close relationship. Over the years, Daddy performed the funeral service for David's daddy and the wedding when David married his wife, Hayley. David is the son my parents never had and the brother I always wanted.

David and Hayley would show up that morning to be there with me. David did many things that week that most people never knew. He helped me gather all of Daddy's guns so that they wouldn't be left in an empty house. One firearm in particular, the last pistol that Daddy held, needed to be taken. I didn't want to touch it. I couldn't. David took it and told me later that cleaning it was the hardest thing he has ever had to do. He also said he would store everything for me until I was ready to get them back. I learned from him later that he destroyed that pistol, and I was glad.

He also helped me dispose of the mattress on Daddy's bed. I hadn't thought much about that until Mr. Fine mentioned it with concern. The emergency workers and men from the funeral home had flipped the mattress over after they took Daddy's body. I went in and put on the comforter, and I hadn't thought about it, but as the week passed, I made a call to David, and he met me at the house. We hauled the mattress away, and a part of what happened went along with it. This was helping to start another healing process.

Elaine—Daddy's oldest niece (as Daddy often referred to her, although she didn't much care for the "oldest" description). They would always laugh about this comment. Elaine was a few years younger than Daddy. Daddy's brother, who was Elaine's father and my uncle, was seventeen years older than my daddy. Uncle Junior is what I called him. He later married my Aunt Delta, and they had seven children together. Daddy had a huge network of nieces and nephews, and the list continued through all their families. Elaine would ignite the family network to let them know about their Uncle Joe Bob.

Elaine would later take Barney, Daddy's dog, to live with her. We were all so worried about what would happen to Barney, so when Elaine requested that we consider her, it was done. She said, "People often say that when they die they would like to come back as a dog, and not just any dog—ELAINE's dog." Those people are right.

David (our preacher)—David would ignite the other side of our family's network and our church friends. David was one of Daddy's nephews and the preacher of the church that I had recently started attending. He preached Momma's funeral, and he would be preaching this one. I needed to hear some words from him. I needed to feel God around me. I needed help finding him. I needed someone to pray with me.

When David got to the house, I ran out and hugged him. I was going to be at church that morning, and none of this was supposed to be happening. We shared tears and made our way into the house, passing by Daddy's desk. As we were making our way in, I saw Daddy's Bible on his desk. I grabbed it. I turned around to David who was walking behind me, and with both hands I pushed the Bible into his chest.

"Romans 8:28, Romans 8:28, Romans 8:28, this was Daddy's favorite verse, and I want you to use that verse and Daddy's Bible with his notes to prepare the funeral message. Will you do that?"

I remember giving this directive, but I didn't know why. David told me later that he was taken back a bit because this wasn't a commonly used verse for funerals. He would even share with the congregation at the funeral how difficult it was for him to use this verse for his uncle's situation. He said I was "pretty assertive" in my request.

And we know that all things work together
for good to them that love God, to them who
are the called according to his purpose.
—Romans 8:28

Something came over me in that moment, in the moment when I passed by Daddy's Bible. It spoke to me. I could hear all his sermons, his fatherly advice, and everything that was my daddy's voice came through in that instant. It was Daddy, using me to spread a message that he knew now to be absolute. "All things work together for good," because Daddy was on the other side now. He was soaked in the truth of those words.

My friends, new and old, have been with me anytime my life has been completely shaken to its core. I don't speak with some of them often, yet when I fall to my knees, there they are. I am surrounded by my sweet, loving, understanding, and unconditional friendships. When life is cold and lonely, I have their arms to wrap around me and hold me together. They are my stitches when I have an open wound and a broken heart. They are the healing that only friends can provide. They are part of yet another invisible scar.

If you are short on the friend list, be a friend. "It takes one to know one" is right. All it takes to increase your friendships is to be a friend. Be the friend who you would want to have in your life. Be the friend whom others turn to in times of tragedy. In doing so, you will be surrounded by their love in your times of need. I've had a lot of those times. Three years has been a long time for tragedy to last, but as far as a friendship is concerned, it's only a second. The love you have given will be returned, and it feels so good.

They say "friends are the family you choose," and I have chosen some pretty amazing ones. I have reconnected with friends from my past and connected with new ones. The love that a friend offers you is unlike any other. It's not required, it's not obligatory, it's just love. It's from the heart. It's beautiful.

Beautiful.

There's that word again.

Think Points

☐ If you're part of someone's support network, and they are dealing with a loss, do your best to stay present and consistent to what you were doing before the loss. If you were a friend, stay a friend. Don't avoid them because it's a tough topic. It may feel a little difficult at first, but just let them know you are there for them. They are going to need you. The loneliest times are *months* after the loss when reality starts to sink in. For some, the first year is the hardest. For others, it may be the second or third year. There is no rule or answer on what will be hardest for someone.

☐ We are all completely different in our grief.
    Things you can do:
- Share quick texts, calls, or notes to let them know you are thinking of them.
- Offer to take them out or for a walk.
- Avoid asking for things that may put pressure on them.
- Don't ask, "How can I help?" Instead say, "May I mow your lawn?" Be specific with your offer to help.

☐ Avoid offering comparisons. Remember, my grief is not like yours.

....
....
....

12

The "D" Diets: Death, Divorce, and Discovery

. . . he that cometh to me shall never hunger;
and he that believeth on me shall never thirst.
—John 6:35

WHEN WE LOSE SOMEONE, whether it's to death or divorce, our body mourns with us, affecting our diet and exercise. Neither of those words is my favorite—diet or exercise. What I am attempting to explain is that what happens in our life can be directly reflected in the food we eat or don't eat. I found myself discovering food was not only important, but an important part of how I was feeling on the inside.

In divorce, you often stop eating because the one you were eating with or cooking for is gone. So, what's the point? In death, you either eat less, eat nothing, or eat more than you have eaten before. Food represents many different things to us—comfort, pain, hurt, loss, stability, uncertainty, reward, punishment, or maybe all these things. The key to our health is the gentle balance that we must return to when our equilibrium is shattered.

Sometimes in a new relationship, we experience similar food issues, but from pure joy and excitement. I like to call that "flitterpated." *Flitterpated: Extremely unable to process simple daily routines, thoughts, or anything and everything because the mind is in a constant state of turmoil, balancing normal function with a genuine passion and absolute infatuation with someone.* We don't eat because we may be trying to fit into that cute little black dress or we overeat because we are just so damn happy. In the situation with new love, you can't go wrong. Why? It's happiness and hope! Hope that is in store for everyone who is open to it. It's out there, but you must get through the darkness to see its light. So hopefully you will soon be *flitterpated* and enjoying food once again.

In death, it can never be predicted how you will react to food. I never knew that the body was capable of shutting down your appetite, but it will. I was shutting down and shutting out anything that had brought me any comfort before.

Understanding the "D" diets chapter will help you to be aware and prepare for what is to come. I hope you never experience the negative results that come with the death and divorce diet, but if you do, I hope this chapter helps you. The Discovery diet is what you can look forward to. Discover the beauty of life in every bite and discover a new you.

The Death Diet

I am all too familiar with the fellowship that food provides. It is a highlight, a necessity, and as crucial to fellowship as the preacher is to Sunday morning services.

Food is a constant in life. It's necessary. When Momma died, so did my appetite. I couldn't eat; I couldn't *think* of eating. I didn't want it. It upset me when other people would eat. *How could they?* Food was not on my list. If Momma wasn't cooking, I wasn't going to eat. She was gone and so was any thought of ever wanting to eat again.

I was nauseous most of the time. I craved water, iced or lukewarm, it didn't matter. I was thirstier than I have ever been in my life. I wanted nothing else. I read where the increase in adrenaline from stress can cause the body to dehydrate rapidly, which explains the cotton mouth and need of excess water. Give me that H_2O!

Anyone who knows me well knows that I'm an advocate for water. "Drink water," I would say to my daughter and to Daddy repeatedly. As a schoolteacher, I realized that water helps your brain. Studies show that water helps improve your mood, helps you focus, and can help you fall asleep faster and sleep deeper. Well, those are things that we can all benefit from, no matter our circumstances. I probably drank a few gallons a day during the first week after the accident. Later, the water would turn to wine. I didn't drink gallons of wine, but I did enjoy a glass or two, or sometimes three.

I remember sitting outside on the bench in my parents' front yard a few weeks after Momma's death. Daddy came out to sit beside me. I had a glass of merlot in a small paper cup. Daddy leaned over and sniffed my cup. I laughed a little because Daddy liked to smell everything. I said, "It's wine, Daddy." He said, "Well, that's all right. Just don't let it become too much."

In that moment, Daddy and I bonded over what is commonplace to so many. He allowed me that moment, that drink, without correction and without forbidding it. I understood and respected his feelings about alcohol, or the lack of. As an adult, I have come to enjoy a nice glass of wine.

Whether I had wine or water, I still didn't want food. From the evening of July 29 to August 5, just seven days, I lost seven pounds. I remember eating one sandwich during that week. A sweet neighbor lady had brought some wonderful ham and cheese sandwiches, heated on Hawaiian rolls with poppyseed dressing. I reached over all the other food that had been left by so many and pulled one square out of the bunch, which were nestled inside aluminum foil. It was delicious, and I will never forget how it tasted. I felt as if I was betraying Momma by eating food and enjoying it. I felt that any type of pleasure should be avoided. She couldn't eat anymore, so neither should I, but that sandwich really was good.

During grief, you will feel guilt over the simplest of life's pleasures. I didn't think eating should be something to enjoy anymore. I felt I didn't deserve it. Grief will implant guilt in all the places that it doesn't belong. For some, food is what you turn to in times of hurt, stress, or anguish. For me, it wasn't.

The week of Momma's funeral, food was brought to Daddy's house in abundance. Barbecue, chicken, so much fried chicken, casseroles, sandwiches, lasagna, salads, fruit, cobblers, pies, cakes, cookies—anything and everything. It was so nice and thoughtful. That is how people showed their love for us, especially here in the South.

Momma had cooked and taken food to people for fifty years in that community—death, marriage, sickness, church fellowship, and any prayer service or peanut farmer gathering that Daddy had planned. Momma was a machine in the kitchen. She could cater the entire event, and she often did. So this is how the community gave back to Daddy and showed their sympathy for his pain, for our pain.

When Daddy passed, when I found him, when I saw death, I began the death diet all over again. Given the circumstances of Daddy's death, it should be pretty self-explanatory why I couldn't eat. But even more than that, it was that the one person I had left on this earth was gone, the one parent, that is. It's that simple. I was alone.

I couldn't eat, but when I think back on it, I found myself being a little stubborn about it. I was bothered when I saw people eating. I felt that their ability to eat something was disrespecting my loss, the pain I was in. *We should all be fasting!* That is the thought that kept going through my head. But that's not right. We should be healing!

I remember when I crashed the Ranger into the plow under the grass and had to get stitches to heal the open wound. I didn't let it stay open and bleeding. I got a doctor to stitch me up so that my skin could bond back together and heal, creating a small scar. Our loss is the new open wound, and we must allow it to heal. We need food to give our body nourishment in order to help us get back to a normal balance within. You will have a scar—we all have different scars in different stages of healing, but you are healing within, and you will soon see it.

Looking back, Momma cooked food, Daddy ate food, and my parents witnessed with food. Food was a way to show their love and the love of God. Taking food baskets to families in need for Thanksgiving and Christmas was just one more way to show Christ's love for us.

Turkeys, hams, and bags of fruit with nuts and candy canes can do a lot for a family that otherwise would have nothing on the table. Momma would also add in her homemade peanut brittle. *DELICIOUS!* She made this in huge batches and would break it so it would fit into gallon Ziploc bags. She put all the bags in a big basket and gave everyone at church one for Christmas. Although I can make the recipe, and it tastes very similar, I have yet to master the ability to make it in the quantities that Momma did. I'm not the machine that she was, but I'm a close second.

Finding your balance with food is going to help you in your healing journey. You may not even be able to think about a healing journey right now, and that's okay. Just think about a sandwich—two pieces of bread, a little slice of ham or turkey, maybe even a slice of cheese. Now, just eat it. Don't think, just eat. And don't forget to drink your water.

The Divorce Diet

It's not as common, but I was on all three diets at one time. My death and divorce diets intertwined, and I was discovering myself all at the same time. From the time Momma was killed on the farm until I found Daddy on Father's Day morning, I was on the divorce diet. I just didn't know it. This diet can change daily, depending on the relationship status between a husband and wife. Many of you may have experienced the divorce diet. It's a common plan that more than 50 percent of the adult married population will sign up for, whether they realize they are on it or not. It's an automatic enrollment. You separate, file for divorce, and bingo—the divorce diet and exercise begin.

The diet works in a variety of ways. You are not hungry at all, or you eat but can't keep it down, for that matter. Some people will turn to excessive exercise. Getting those endorphins to help mask our pain and create good feelings is a source of pleasure that is missing now. This plan is good for a new dress size or in preparing one to begin the search for a new mate. Just as you are not able to eat during a divorce, you are simultaneously being eaten alive by the stress on your body, mind, and spirit.

My divorce diet came in two parts. One started just eight days after my mother's funeral when I found out my husband was talking to another woman. I had been staying with Daddy, helping him adjust to his new world. It was such a blessing to get this time with Daddy, but what I didn't and couldn't imagine was at the end of those six weeks, I might be returning to an empty house.

I had a wonderful substitute who was doing a long-term assignment with my classes. Everything was coming together to get me through this time, and to get Daddy through this time. I would send video messages to all my students on how excited I was to see them soon. I was very open with my kids, as they were all young adults. They gave me some of the best comfort and advice during this time.

"Take it not only one day at a time, but one hour and one step."

"Be thankful for what you still DO have."

"You can do this! You are the strongest teacher I know. You carry yourself so well for having gone through so much."

I hadn't even met them, and they were giving me the best advice I had ever received. Out of the mouths of babes—or sixteen-year-olds—they were still welcomed words for my ears.

During the time that I was getting affirmation from my high school students and fellow teachers, I was getting the opposite from my husband. I was left to feel guilty for "leaving our home" and "never coming back." I did just lose my mother in a horrific way, but maybe I should or could have dealt with the cards differently. There were many choices, and we each had to choose our own path. I thought our relationship was stronger than it actually was. Death brings lasting darkness with it, and sometimes it's disguised so we never see it until it's too late.

Many people would ask, "How are you and your husband doing?" as if they sensed a strain in our marriage. I took my spouse's commitment to me and our marriage for granted. "We are good. Our marriage is so much stronger than this." I genuinely believed it was, but it wasn't.

It wasn't.

My husband became increasingly agitated when talking with me during those six weeks. He would call and be upset, or he wouldn't call. I remember hearing Daddy call and leave him a voice mail one evening, just as I had gotten out of the shower. Whispering, Daddy said, "Can you please call Thelizabeth? She needs and misses you." I acted like I didn't hear him. Daddy felt guilty for so many things and my marriage was one of them. He was doing what he could, even in his grief, to try to help, but the marriage was already broken. It had been for a while. The grief just brought it to the surface.

"Grief separates the adults from the children," Gale had told me during one of my visits. My texts, appointments, and phone calls with Gale increased when I found out that my husband had been talking to another woman. I immediately texted Gale in a panic. She called me. Later that week, I went to see her for an official counseling session. "You are going through so much right now that I don't think you can handle one more thing." She meant a divorce.

She was right.

When I found out about the affair, or affairs, my stomach sank. I felt faint. I was grieving Momma, living with Daddy through the adjustment, all while my husband was finding comfort in the arms of someone else. I felt like the world, my world, was being completely taken away from me. I felt lower than ever before. The hits to my stomach kept coming, one after another. One for grief and another for a failing marriage, hit after hit.

When a marriage is falling apart, you lose your closest support system. I didn't have the person I had always turned to, and any love I longed for was gone. Most of all, I didn't have Momma to get advice from. It was all gone, falling, crashing, crumbling.

Where was she? God, I can't handle all this. It's all too much. She was supposed to be here. I needed to talk to her about everything that was happening. I decided to write her a note, even though I knew she would never read it.

Momma,

I don't think he loves me anymore.

Oh Momma, it's all fading away. I need to feel you again. I can't do this. I can't do any of this without you. I have never felt so alone.

Please come back to me, however you can. Please, oh please, Momma. I'm breaking and dying inside. I can't be as strong as you. I can't live without you. I can't be what I need to be without you. I need you. Please come back.

I feel like I am dying with you.

I love you, Momma,
Thelizabeth

I was betrayed by the one I had loved, while in my most vulnerable and weakest state, and the pattern continued over the next three years. We were both filling the void in our lives, but in very different ways.

I had put off telling Daddy anything about what was going on within my marriage, but I knew I couldn't continue to act out the charade. A few weeks before Daddy died, I took him breakfast and stayed to talk while we drank our coffee. I was always holding back tears since Momma died, and I was damn good at it. I could hold back my hurt so well that I should have received an Oscar for my performance. I played a girl who was unaffected by the loss of her mom; her husband and her life were perfect.

I hadn't planned it. But this time, I told Daddy. It just happened. Daddy asked again about my husband. I replied, "Well, I need to talk to you about that."

Immediately, Daddy said, "What? Is it bad?" He knew. He just knew.

"Daddy, he left me, and we are getting a divorce."

"Uhhhh, no." Daddy was upset, letting out a moan and sigh. I assured him I was okay and that we were all going to be okay. I didn't want him to think I was falling apart. I didn't want Daddy to know the truth about how I was feeling. The truth was, Daddy knew the whole time. Why is it that we hide how we feel? We all do it, but our bodies can only hold so much, and our eyes usually give us away. The windows to our soul can't lie.

I wanted to go fall on him crying and ask him to make it all better, but I couldn't. I just couldn't. I had to be tough, still. I had to be strong for Daddy. It would only be eleven more days that Daddy would have to live with that truth. Only eleven more days.

Maybe I shouldn't have told him. *Damn!* The guilt after a suicide will eat you alive if you let it. I had to seek counseling, friends, and my faith to control my self-blame of why I told him. *Why?* I learned it is not something that I did or didn't do. It was what he needed to do. It was nobody's fault—there was no one to blame.

The Discovery Diet

To eat or not to eat—that is the question. If you are able to find a balance, this diet will do you well. Balance is everything. If I have learned one thing, it is that balance is key. Try to control yourself if you are overeating due to stress from loss. I realize this is so easy for me to suggest but hear me out.

Now, what do we do about the lack of or overconsumption from stress and fatigue? If you don't realize it now, you eventually will. Food isn't the problem. Whether food is the comfort or the aggravation, it is still just that—food. Sustenance. A provision that is required for life. Food is what we must have to survive.

I learned so much about my body during these life-altering events. I learned that what we associate with food is what we hope to get from food. I wanted my life back, my parents back, my marriage back, all the way they once were. For that reason, I didn't eat. I couldn't. You would think that I would eat to try to bring them back with my memory of the food, but I was physically sickened by the thought of food. My association with food formed as a child. It was love, happiness, fellowship, togetherness. It wasn't this. It wasn't loneliness. It wasn't what this was. In other words, eat and understand what that physical act is, not what it isn't.

Commonly referred to as eating disorders, or disordered eating, I was unaware it was happening. I had to discover that food was food, and regardless of how I felt about things going on in my life, food was a necessity.

You will DISCOVER you in this process. The process is you. You and nothing else. You and faith. I had hit the rock bottom of loneliness. It was just me and God now, for real. Oh, and my dog. I had my dog, Manly—he was still eating.

I had lost my inner circle. Momma was gone, my counselor was gone, my husband was gone, and now Daddy was gone. I now had what I once feared the most—losing those I love and being alone.

I had my daughter, but she was busy in law school. I had my friends, but they had their own lives, although without them I don't think I could have withstood the waves of loss that were drowning me. My friends were the rope pulling me back in, the life raft being sent to save me. This book was open, and they knew I'd been working on it. They knew it needed to be completed. The support, love, and encouragement they gave led me on the road to discovery.

I discovered who I am. Everything that I thought defined who I was had been taken away, and I was left with my fears and my faith. I discovered that I am a child of God who needed him, and I leaned on him.

I prayed.

I ate.

I would love again.

Your faith can lead you on the discovery diet. You will pray again. You will eat again. You will love again. You won't be looking for it. It will find you and grab you, leaving you breathless. Be open to it. Let hope grab you. Let hope take your breath away. It will be the best thing you have felt in a long time.

I remember years ago, after church, we were all eating lunch at the kitchen table in my old house. Sunday lunch was an event. Momma always made the main meal, and it was always heavenly. I made the dessert. It was fun to decide what different delight to prepare each Saturday before. For this meal, I had made a creamy banana pudding, one of Daddy's favorites. This recipe was Momma's, made with Eagle Brand Sweetened Condensed Milk and Cool Whip, a slight taste of lemon on the bananas to prevent discoloring, and the result was de-licous!

I looked over at Momma with tears in my eyes and said, "One day we won't all be right here." It was as if foreshadowing had come to me in an instant. I stopped eating my mashed potatoes and meatloaf and realized that one day we wouldn't be in our spots. Daddy on my right, Momma on my left, and my daughter in her highchair in front of me. I knew that it wouldn't last, but I was so scared of this thought that I had to say it out loud to hear some words of comfort from Momma to help me. She smiled, reached her hand out to mine, and said, "Well, that's just life. Now, eat your food."

She was right.

That's just life. Now, eat your food.

Think Points

☐ For helping to get through the "D" Diets, try placing Post-it notes around your house reminding you to "drink water" or "eat a sandwich" or "take a walk."

☐ What can you do to help others when they are experiencing the death or divorce diet?

Here are a few ideas. A friend of mine writes positive and encouraging words on water bottles while helping put them away in the refrigerator.

You may consider inviting them out to lunch.

You may offer to help portion out and freeze the excess food people have given, so they can eat it at a later date.

....

....

....

....

....

....

....

....

....

....

....

....

....

13

In the Room

Never underestimate the power of being
present, the beauty of being.
—Theo Boyd

218 MY GRIEF IS NOT LIKE YOURS

In March 2018, I took Momma to a women's conference in Dallas. We didn't get great seats, but we were in the middle section, halfway back in a group with about 2,300 other people. I was hoping there would be a monitor for captioning or even a person performing sign language, but there wasn't.

I looked at Momma and moved my lips to silently say I was sorry that she couldn't hear anything the speakers were saying. She said, "It's okay. I'm just happy to be in the room."

When I was about nine, and the annual piano recital was approaching. Momma was in the kitchen washing dishes and preparing for the next meal. When I needed her to listen to one of my piano pieces, knowing she couldn't hear my fingers hit the keys didn't matter. I just needed her there.

Looking back, I cannot imagine how tired she was, having worked with Daddy all day on the farm. I had been practicing the piano music that I was going to perform, and I asked her several times to come and listen, come be in the room. It is one of the only times that I saw and felt her frustration. It was a feeling I would never be able to understand because I took it for granted that I could hear my fingers hit the keys and she couldn't.

I persisted in my childish ignorance. She dried her hands on the worn kitchen towel and came in the room. It was there that she would sit and pretend she could hear me play. She never said anything about my mistakes, but she did offer some of the best advice I have ever received. "Sit up and be strong. Don't show me when you mess up. Just keep going." This echo was familiar. My piano teacher, Mrs. Bessire, told me something very similar. "Make your mistakes loud," she'd say as she caught my posture falling, my shoulders shrugging, or my lips pursing from a few keys that were mistakenly hit by my nervous fingers.

Having spent a lifetime in a silent world, Momma had become an expert at being. Being present. Being there. Being in the room. When I was sick and stayed home from school, she was there, sitting on the end of my twin bed, running her hands up and down my leg or lying beside me. Her presence was felt.

During the night, if I was sick or feeling bad, I could never call out for Momma. She took her hearing aid out at night so even the smallest amount of sound she had available to her disappeared. If I felt bad, I had to call for Daddy. He would get up and help us, whether that was bringing me a glass of water, cleaning me if I had thrown up, or just telling a story to soothe me back to sleep. Later, Momma would be upset that Daddy didn't wake her up. She told me once that she felt she missed out on part of motherhood by not hearing us each time we might have needed her. I assured her that she only missed out on those gross parts. She was there for everything beautiful, no matter how disguised it may have been.

Having thought about this so many times since then, the power of that statement has never left me: "in the room." Most of us can hear, and often we are not even in the room. We skip, dodge, and even lie to avoid being present in a moment when someone may need us the most. When was the last time you sat in a room by yourself without distraction, quiet and still? Maybe you do this in prayer or meditation, or perhaps you never stop long enough to even try.

Momma was deaf; she couldn't hear anything that was said, but she was present. She was in the room. She always was, no matter what it cost her. Never doubt the importance of being present, whether it is to help someone or just for yourself. Remember, sometimes it's not about anything but being in the room.

The last time I was in the room with Momma, all I could do was think about all the times she had been there for me. She modeled perfection for being present, no matter when, where, or what the situation may have been. All the years of my life summarized in that short time I was with her for the last time. What was so familiar during this time was her silence. She was always there. I was there. Daddy and my sister were there. We sat with her for hours. She was once again the strength in my being, the push that I needed, the love that gave me wings. She was in the room.

My sister sang Celine Dion's "Because You Loved Me" at Momma's funeral. The words in that song say what Momma did so effortlessly, so inherently. I am only who I am because she loved me. She.

> *You were my strength when I was weak.*
> *You were my voice when I couldn't speak.*
> *You were my eyes when I couldn't see.*
> *You saw the best there was in me.*
> **—recorded by Celine Dion and**
> **written by Diane Warren**

Whether he realized it or not, Daddy was also an expert at being in the room. Daddy's room was larger. His presence was overpowering at times. He commanded a room, whereas Momma's presence was a subtle sway in a soft section of space. Daddy was a powerful force felt by everyone immediately. In the pulpit he was respected and listened to. He was the leader. Momma was his cheerleader. The last time I was in the room with Daddy, he was still the wind beneath my wings, pushing me to be better and move forward. Only this time, he was at peace, silent, and with Momma.

As I sit here writing to you, I realize that I have learned how to live from two of the best examples life had to offer—Sue and Joe Bob, my momma and daddy. They were the most important and necessary ingredients for a story to have meaning and be the testimony needed to help others when they feel they are in sinking sand.

These two extraordinary human beings gave me a foundation grounded in Jesus, sprinkled with peanuts, and topped with love.

A REMEMBRANCE EXERCISE

Please don't forget me.
—Joe Bob Boyd

I CAME UP WITH THIS exercise when thoughts of Momma kept popping in my head continually. I grabbed my laptop and started pecking away at the keyboard. We do not have to do what society dictates to us or what others may think is best. We know what we are feeling, so feel it.

Just three years later, I found myself doing this again, but for Daddy. I want to remember them both. I just kept thinking of things about Daddy, so I started jotting down what I remember about him until I reached one hundred.

When Daddy was near his end, although we didn't realize how close, he seemed to be concerned that he would one day be forgotten. This man, larger than life, was so worried that his life, his work, his existence wouldn't be remembered. This book, this exercise, and my mission to help others is all a testament to my parents, who they were and who they made—me.

I urge you to do the same for the person you are grieving. All you need is a pen or pencil, a piece of paper, a keyboard, or your phone. Don't worry about a chronological order; just start with the first, second, third things that come into your head and stop at one hundred, or you can keep going.

100 Things about Momma

1. Momma was beautiful.
2. Momma was confident.
3. Momma had 2 sisters.
4. Momma was deaf.
5. Momma was a size 4.
6. Momma had naturally wavy hair.
7. Momma always wore fashionable clothes.
8. Momma had 1 husband.
9. Momma was timelessly elegant.
10. Momma tucked me in at night.
11. Momma was smart.
12. Momma went to college.
13. Momma loved her home.
14. Momma cooked the best food.
15. Momma baked the most delicious pies.
16. Momma never complained.
17. Momma loved my daughter.
18. Momma helped me raise my daughter.
19. Momma loved animals.
20. Momma was so gracious.
21. Momma was so kind.

22. Momma was educated.
23. Momma loved blue.
24. Momma loved pink.
25. Momma loved her mom.
26. Momma loved her dad.
27. Momma loved sewing.
28. Momma sewed all our clothes when I was young.
29. Momma sewed my prom dresses.
30. Momma sewed for others.
31. Momma was hypoglycemic.
32. Momma was neat.
33. Momma was polished.
34. Momma was classy.
35. Momma was strong.
36. Momma worked on a farm.
37. Momma drove a tractor.
38. Momma loved my dad.
39. Momma loved her daughters.
40. Momma loved her grandchildren.
41. Momma loved to cook for people.
42. Momma loved sharing her story.
43. Momma had a hard childhood.
44. Momma was sexually abused as a child.
45. Momma didn't hear anything until she was ten years old.
46. Momma laughed.
47. Momma ate healthy food.
48. Momma exercised.
49. Momma loved dressing up.
50. Momma spoke.

51. Momma had good teachers.
52. Momma was a cheerleader in high school.
53. Momma wore shoulder pads in the 1980s.
54. Momma taught me how to wash my face each night.
55. Momma taught me about Jesus.
56. Momma loved Jesus.
57. Momma said, "God is a mystery."
58. Momma loved her new car.
59. Momma would forgive.
60. Momma was patient.
61. Momma had a Bible.
62. Momma took us to church with Daddy.
63. Momma was a preacher's wife.
64. Momma was a farmer's wife.
65. Momma loved to bake.
66. Momma shelled black eyed peas faster than anyone.
67. Momma was bitten by a copperhead snake.
68. Momma killed a snake.
69. Momma burned brush and cleared log jams.
70. Momma delivered many calves with Daddy.
71. Momma had beautiful skin.
72. Momma wore hats.
73. Momma did what the doctors told her.
74. Momma had beautiful handwriting.
75. Momma had stitches in her right hand once from a broken glass she was washing.
76. Momma didn't get a dishwasher until 2014.

77. Momma had a high fever when she was a baby.
78. Momma's middle name was Wynell.
79. Momma didn't like her middle name.
80. Momma loved to watercolor.
81. Momma loved to watch *Dancing with the Stars*.
82. Momma loved to decorate her Christmas tree.
83. Momma loved to take pictures.
84. Momma loved to watch bowling.
85. Momma loved to sew.
86. Momma loved to bake.
87. Momma loved to cook.
88. Momma loved to can food.
89. Momma loved to hang clothes on a line.
90. Momma loved the smell of a clean house.
91. Momma loved to take a shower and put on her pajamas.
92. Momma made the best food ever!
93. Momma had patience for everything.
94. Momma was a nanny in the 1960s in Dallas and California.
95. Momma couldn't hear, write, or speak until she was ten years old.
96. Momma was killed on the farm.
97. Momma loved Daddy.
98. Momma was unlike any other person in my life that I have or ever will meet.
99. Momma knew how to do anything.
100. Momma loved me.

100 Things about Daddy

1. Daddy loved me.
2. Daddy loved my sister.
3. Daddy loved Momma.
4. Daddy loved his grandchildren.
5. Daddy loved talking.
6. Daddy loved laughing.
7. Daddy loved telling jokes.
8. Daddy loved writing.
9. Daddy loved animals.
10. Daddy loved poetry.
11. Daddy loved dirt.
12. Daddy loved peanuts.
13. Daddy loved cherries.
14. Daddy loved chocolate.
15. Daddy loved eating.
16. Daddy loved food.
17. Daddy knew the Bible.
18. Daddy loved preaching.
19. Daddy loved teaching.
20. Daddy loved singing.
21. Daddy loved Floyd Cramer's piano playing.
22. Daddy loved Patsy Cline.
23. Daddy loved Loretta Lynn.
24. Daddy loved Buddy Holly.
25. Daddy loved the 1950s.
26. Daddy loved his 1956 Ford car.
27. Daddy loved old stuff.
28. Daddy loved the old days.

29. Daddy loved his girlfriends from high school.
30. Daddy loved all his friends.
31. Daddy loved homemade Big Red ice cream.
32. Daddy loved the fall.
33. Daddy loved growing watermelons and selling them out of his truck.
34. Daddy loved working each Christmas ringing the bell for the Salvation Army.
35. Daddy helped me with my homework.
36. Daddy always listened to me.
37. Daddy loved to talk on the phone.
38. Daddy loved to eat popcorn.
39. Daddy loved to watch *Coal Miner's Daughter.*
40. Daddy loved to eat at restaurants.
41. Daddy loved bread.
42. Daddy loved red beans.
43. Daddy loved helping others.
44. Daddy loved his parents.
45. Daddy loved his Bible.
46. Daddy loved church.
47. Daddy loved being a Christian.
48. Daddy loved being a father.
49. Daddy loved being a husband.
50. Daddy loved his sisters.
51. Daddy loved his brother.
52. Daddy loved his nieces and nephews.
53. Daddy loved his dog Barney.
54. Daddy loved all his pets.
55. Daddy had a horse named Paint.
56. Daddy loved to be outside.

57. Daddy loved peanut brittle.
58. Daddy loved Momma's cooking.
59. Daddy loved being a farmer.
60. Daddy loved being a rancher.
61. Daddy loved being a leader.
62. Daddy loved school.
63. Daddy loved learning.
64. Daddy loved his home.
65. Daddy loved the land.
66. Daddy loved staying home.
67. Daddy loved cotton candy.
68. Daddy loved Long John Silver's.
69. Daddy loved taking us to the zoo when we were little.
70. Daddy loved football games.
71. Daddy loved playing football.
72. Daddy loved his youth.
73. Daddy loved his childhood.
74. Daddy loved his best friend, Stanley.
75. Daddy loved playing in the woods as a boy.
76. Daddy loved writing about his life.
77. Daddy loved preaching a funeral.
78. Daddy loved writing short stories.
79. Daddy has two published short stories.
80. Daddy has one published poem.
81. Daddy loved helping anyone who needed help.
82. Daddy loved Coke and root beer.
83. Daddy loved pork chops.
84. Daddy loved cake.

85. Daddy loved Momma's cooking.
86. Daddy loved all of his family.
87. Daddy loved to pick up hitchhikers.
88. Daddy loved to talk to people.
89. Daddy loved 18-wheelers.
90. Daddy loved watching TV.
91. Daddy loved *The Lone Ranger.*
92. Daddy loved writing.
93. Daddy was the best daddy.
94. Daddy was the best husband.
95. Daddy was the best son.
96. Daddy was good at everything he did.
97. Daddy loved life.
98. Daddy was sad.
99. Daddy was strong.
100. Daddy is in Heaven.

It isn't about the order of your memory—it's about what you remember. It's about writing it down. Knowing these are your memories and letting them flow freely without judgment is what this exercise is about. This is your list, and it belongs to you. If you want to share it, then share it. If you want to keep it only for yourself, then keep it. If Momma and Daddy read this, they would probably blush, and that makes me smile.

My parents are so much a part of who I am that once I finished my lists of one hundred things, it became more about who I am and not as much about them. Sometimes the very thing that people are trying to discourage you from doing or talking about is the very thing you need to exist. Don't be afraid to be strong. Don't be afraid to talk about them.

Keep them alive with your memories.

REMEMBERING HER

Words I Spoke at My Mother's Funeral
August 3, 2019

https://open.spotify.com/episode/7fFLSMDcW7HOM
jTqkbETKs?si=cff22d0d87f74a8e

[Music plays] When being in the presence of my mom, you automatically felt better. You never left without a smile on your face or on hers. She flowed through life like water in a stream: gentle, constant, pushing harder after a rain, but slowing just enough for us all to see her grace and beauty. [sniffles]

[Music plays] Some of these things you may know, and some things you may not know. Can everybody hear me okay? My mother loved art, and she was an artist in many ways: drawing, painting, sketching. She loved water coloring. She went to classes, and I think she was so good she even was a threat to the teacher. [laughter] She drew many nativity scenes through the years for the church; top to bottom nativity. I mean, the animals, the stable, the manger. No one ever believed that just my mom did that. Her cursive handwriting, I've never seen anything like it. Even a grocery store list was written with deliberate intention.

She was a meticulous seamstress and tailor. She sewed, mended, created many, if not all, of our clothes through the years, prom dresses, church dresses, drill team uniforms, my Glinda the Good Witch dress, [laughter] graduation, piano recital formals, and even sewed cushions. She sewed so seamlessly that people were in awe that it wasn't something from Neiman Marcus. And after all night of sewing, our dresses for church would be hanging in our room ready for us the next Sunday morning. In this respect as well, she could take a men's dress shirt apart for Daddy to try on in the store and put it exactly back in the way it came, pins, cardboard, and everything. [laughter]

It was fascinating. And for her clothes she looked beautiful in blue jeans and work shirts. She would even iron her work shirts. She took so much pride in the clothes and appearance of her family.

This last week my sister and I found her wedding dress hanging in the guest room closet. It had been to the cleaners recently. She was going to surprise us and have her picture made in it in January for their 50th because she could still fit in her wedding dress. [laughter]

She was famous. She was once held by Elvis Presley. She attended a concert at a young age, and when Elvis heard that she could not hear, he picked her up and patted her on her head, her headband fell over her eyes, and he lifted it up and kissed her. [awws] Not only would the Elvis part make her famous, last night I think it was pretty evident she's famous.

Her cooking. I think most of you in this room know that my mother was a master chef of not just Hill County, but this entire state. Her pies were fought over, her peanut brittle addictive and coveted by all, and there was never a time you never left her home hungry. She fed the sick, the grieving, ministers, visitors, and we did entire catering jobs for church events and Daddy's peanut farmer get-togethers. She loved cooking.

She was a master gardener and snake killer. [laughter] She was bitten by a copperhead snake almost three years ago, and here recently, she killed one and made Daddy take her picture with it. [laughter] She was the Crocodile Dundee of Hill County. She herded cattle, horses, and even buffalo a few times. Her favorite garden tools were the weed eater and the blower. Daddy said, "If Sue sees a speck of dirt, she's got that blower going." [laughter] She cleared brush and logjams in creeks, chopped down trees, repotted all her plants and remulched the flower beds, and mowed the yard, and that was just one morning. [laughter]

Her art of giving and loving. She gave of herself every moment of her life. She drove my sister and me to piano lessons twice a week for over thirteen years, and yet at each practice or recital she never heard a note. She drove my sister and me to take swimming lessons at Carl's Corner. [laughter]

Yep, they had a pool outside at that time and offered swimming lessons one summer. No one ever believed it when I tell them I learned how to swim at Carl's Corner. [laughter]

She potty-trained all her grandchildren. My sister and I would leave our Reagen and Jonah, and once when we returned to pick them up, voilà! They were magically potty-trained! [laughter] She was currently working on my nephew Henry. [laughter]

She practically raised my Reagen. [sobs] Taught her so many things, and I see my mom in Reagen [sobs] a little more every day. I'm doin' this. [bangs pulpit]

She was a self-esteem booster. She was thankful for everything, and I know she would be thankful for you all today, as we are for her. When being in the presence of my mom, you automatically felt better. You never left without a smile on your face or on hers. She flowed through life like water in a stream, gentle, constant, pushing harder after a rain, but slowing just enough for us all to see her grace and beauty. [congregation sniffles]

[Music plays]

What She Hears

Poem by Thelizabeth Boyd—Mother's Day 2014

Her mother's worry, her father's prayer,
The doctor's hurry, their sad despair.

The fever too high, left damaged ears,
But no need to cry, look what happened through the
    years.

A place to go, her family's friend,
She didn't know how this would end.

A teacher's hand, so strict and stern,
All expected to understand, for her to speak is what
    they yearned.

This teacher's love, so honest and so true,
With help from above, made her brand-new.

She grew up fast and learned her way,
Even with the past and all its gray.

So, when asked the question, "Can your mother hear
    me?"
You had better get a pen, for what she hears—you will
    see . . .

A boy's request for a second date,
Her heart beating fast, it can hardly wait.

A wedding song, their words, "I do."
And so much more to come for Sue.

The pains of birth, her baby's cry,
Brought me to this earth in that April, morning sky.

Her baby's first steps and later a sister too,
The room she painted would be all blue.
The first words we say with kisses on our cheeks,
Still the same to this day, "I love you, Momma."

With her girls growing up, being a farmer and
    preacher's wife,
This kept full her cup and a very busy life.

Now we're all grown, living out our lives,
With children of our own, wondering—how did she
    survive?

Knowing now what mother knew, how precious and
    so dear,
I realize all the heartaches and the woes, are only ours
    to listen and to hear.

So, for a mother, my mother—this is just some of what
    she hears,
My hopes, my dreams, my fears.

She hears more than most, and here on this earth,

She was my host.

REMEMBERING HIM

Words I Spoke at My Father's Funeral
June 25, 2022

https://open.spotify.com/episode/72kRsJ5HrPvdWUN
fJpwBWJ?si=f039c9454f3545c0

[Music plays] This is the first time I'm going to be able to give a speech without Daddy interrupting me. [laughter]

First of all, I want to thank all of you for spending $1,000 to fill up your gas tank to be here. [laughter] Daddy always said, "Get them laughing in the beginning, and then leave them crying." This funeral is going to be just a tad bit longer because I'm eating up some of the preacher's time.

Can everybody hear me okay? Can y'all hear me okay?

Okay. Daddy has a lot of material and content for a character. So for a writer to narrow that down was almost impossible. There was so much material for this speech, that it's shocking that I got it narrowed down, but I did.

Once upon a time there was a little boy born in a community called Bethel. He was not just any boy, as his mother would say, his name was Joe Bob Boyd.

Dr. Treat came over to deliver him because my grandmother had put a white cloth up on the roof. The neighbor ladies would see the cloth and know that it was time. His life was one of the best movies you could ever watch. It's an honor to be the daughter of such a strong character.

A strong character consists of many traits. Let's go over some of these character traits. You've got a school-teacher up here, so get ready.

There were hundreds of character traits for Joe Bob Boyd, and I've narrowed it down to the top ten. Daddy always loved a good top ten.

Number one is hardworking. I felt that weather could fall under this trait. Daddy was consumed with weather, but rightfully so. I've inherited my Daddy's addiction and obsession with the forecast. My daughter just told me last week I'm obsessed with weather.

Rain. I can remember Daddy on the front porch staring at the sky, hoping and praying for rain or for the rain to stop. The crops depended on the balance. He and Momma would have good peanut crop years and bad ones too. In the good years, we would maybe get a few extra school clothes or Momma could get something new. But in the bad ones, we had to be frugal.

My sister and I rode the school bus. Each morning if you stared out the back kitchen window, there was a tiny section in the window and the road that you could see about a mile away and watch for the yellow little dot to pass. We knew that from that yellow strip, we had four to five minutes to get to the bus stop. When it would rain or it was too cold, Daddy would warm up the old pickup and drive us to the stop by the mailbox.

I can remember on two occasions where the school bus got stuck coming up the road to our house. The driver would get out, walk up to Daddy, and say, "Can you pull me out?" Daddy would get his tractor and pull out the school bus.

And being in tune with the weather, crops were always rotating, and in the summer we had to pick watermelons and cantaloupes for money for school clothes.

He grew up in dirt, he loved dirt. He loved what could come from the dirt. He knew and learned agriculture to be the best farmer he could be, and he was. I find it so ironic that he loved the dirt and earth so much, and that is where he will return.

I hear many people say, I wish I had one of Joe Bob's melons, they were the best I ever had. Daddy taught me how to thump them to pick the perfect one, although I'm still not quite sure what sound to look for. I just act like I know what I'm doing, and then when people look at me weird, I just say, "My daddy farmed watermelons and cantaloupes, and I act like an expert."

We would get up at 2 a.m. to take a load of melons we picked the evening before to the Dallas Farmers' Market because Daddy learned that you could get them sold in less than an hour in just one stop. Then we would come back home, stop at McDonald's for breakfast, and go home to sleep. Daddy worked hard building fences, ranching, farming, preaching, and being our daddy and husband to Momma, and helping everyone.

Character trait two: a strong voice. [whistles] That voice! I think everyone in here can recognize Daddy's voice. He used to say, "I don't know why when I call people they know who I am before I even tell 'em!" [laughter] Daddy is the only person I have met that could turn a one-syllable word into three. And the voice was one that was listened to. When Daddy spoke, you listened, or he just got louder. I don't know where I get my voice, but Momma did write in my baby book, "Looks like Daddy. Acts like Daddy. Talks like Daddy."

He wrote stories that he would tell to Hannah and me every night. "Johnny and Snoochie by the Side of the Road" about an orphan brother and sister and their dog. "The Watermelon" about a bully named Billy Bratcher. "Tom Turkey" about a pet turkey that was about to become Thanksgiving lunch. He recorded this one for my third-grade class on a cassette tape, and I got to play that for my class at Thanksgiving break. Last night at visitation, they were remembering Tom Turkey. "This is the story of Tom Turkey." Later on as a teenager. I recorded Duran Duran over that cassette tape and I will forever regret that.

His voice has married, buried, carried almost everyone in Hill County. I'm sure by a show of hands right now in this room, we can see if Daddy has preached a funeral, a wedding, or at one point done a service for you. Please raise your hand.

I couldn't drive Daddy anywhere without hearing, "I preached their funeral. I preached his mom's funeral. I married them. I preached his uncle's funeral. They divorced." He even preached his momma's and daddy's funerals and all his siblings' funerals. His funerals were different. A man here at the funeral home said yesterday when he heard Daddy was going to be the preacher at a funeral, he knew it was going to be a good one.

He wrote poetry. He loved the written word. He carried a 3 by 5 notecard and a pen in his suit or shirt pocket at all times, and when he didn't have a notecard, he would just write on the bottom of his boots. His voice came through in writing, and as a writer he would pour his heart onto the page. And he did this to the very end. I found a box and note cards and so many written treasures this week that I plan to have published and printed to share with all of you and the world. And when Daddy couldn't speak, he would whistle. [whistling] I practiced "Precious Memories." I'm not going to do it.

He had a joke. He said, "What sound does a wolf make?" [Wolf call whistle] [laughter]

Character trait three: funny. Oh, my goodness! Daddy was witty, wise, and funny. Humor got him through all things. Humor was inherited from his daddy, Henry Boyd, and he always made us laugh with his corny jokes. How do you keep a bull from charging? Take away his credit card. What do you call a truckload of pigs? An

18-squealer. What did one tonsil say to the other? Hey, better get ready. I heard Doc's taking us out tonight.

These jokes were a constant in Joe Bob Boyd. I know you all have some of your own memories of Daddy's humor. He loved humor, and it was always with him, even to the end. On Saturday last week, Hannah, as we were leaving, said, "Daddy, which one is the good hand?" He would always do this, "Which one's the good hand?" And he didn't get it at first, but then he pointed and just laughed that famous Daddy laugh. He got it.

Character trait four: considerate and thoughtful. Daddy was constantly considerate, thoughtful, and others was his agenda. He would do anything for anyone at any time. He gave money to complete strangers when we didn't have that much ourselves. He would take food to people that needed it, because he knew if you fed them, helped them, then maybe you could witness to them about the Lord.

He was the Good Samaritan of Hill County. I know this room and beyond is filled with memories of the thoughtful things that Daddy did. One day as a teenager, I had been complaining about picking watermelons and cantaloupe. It was too hot and dirty and sticky, and I didn't want to go. My sister did, and of course Daddy's farm hands that helped him pick melons, they were all picking late into the evening, and a huge Apache helicopter from Fort Hood circled the field. It landed because they were headed to Fort Hood, and they saw the watermelons. Daddy said, "Well, I'll load you up if we can look around in your copter." He loved giving to others and bringing them joy. What a memory! When they got home and told me, I couldn't believe one of the only times I didn't go was army men! [laughter]

Character traits five and six: witty and creative. This could fall under humor, but Daddy had a quick-wittedness about him like no other. Quick comebacks and funny things to say. I felt like nicknames for things would fall under this category. The Big Sissy and the Little Sissy, meaning that if we had the Sissies on, those were our air-conditioners. The Big Sissy was the air conditioner window unit in the living room. The Little Sissy was the window unit in the bedroom. You were sissy if you had to have the air-conditioner on. Often in the summer, we would just turn on the Little Sissy in their room and close the door to the kitchen so the Big Sissy didn't pull as much electricity.

We had almost 150 head of cattle at one time. And Daddy would count these cows with his middle finger, which I never understood. I never understood why Daddy got to use that finger and we weren't supposed to. [laughter] I would stand on the tailgate and sing to the cows, and then when the Sevin Dust went flying, he would just say, "Cover your face!" When my daughter, Reagen, started kindergarten, the teacher contacted me because Reagen was using some farm jargon that she felt might not be appropriate for the class. "That calf was just sucking on his mama's tits." [laughter] And she also drew her farm animal pictures in class anatomically correct,

246 MY GRIEF IS NOT LIKE YOURS

with emphasis on certain parts of the bulls and the cows. [laughter] I told Daddy about it, but he just laughed and said, "Well that's just farm stuff." [laughter]

His cattle had nicknames, the ones that he didn't eat. So here were some of them: Shorthorn for the shorthorn; One Horn, just had one horn; Red Stubby Tits, that one speaks for itself; Satan, mean as the devil. Sunday he delivered that calf after church with his suit on, didn't have time to go home and change. Church got out. Got to deliver it right then. They would spend days walking, looking for a missing calf, or a mama that might be in trouble.

There were so many cattle stories that I'm narrowing it down to one: a twin. And when twin calves are born, the mama often only takes to one, the other one was left for Daddy and Momma and Reagen to bottle feed. They named her Tess, and Daddy kept her longer than any other cow. She was a pet dog-cow to them, and Reagen could go up and pet her and lie with her just like any cat or dog. Tess tugged at Daddy's heartstrings because he knew the sweet memories of Reagan with her. Momma said, "Losing Tess to your Daddy was really hard."

And when Reagen started school, she told me that Bob told her, "Bob said he can learn me anything I need to know, so I don't have to go to school." [laughter]

Character seven: extremely intelligent. Daddy could talk to the homeless man or the seminary scholar. He was the Andy Griffith of Hill County mixed with a little bit of Clint Eastwood, and some Bob Hope. He was so smart that he had seminary professors left speechless with his questions on the Gospel. It was shocking how a self-taught ordained minister knew more than a seminary graduate that had spent their life in seminary school.

His diligence to study the Bible was discipline, which is our next character trait: discipline.

Hannah and I didn't get a choice on whether we got to go to church or not. We went unless we had a fever or were throwing up. Daddy did too. He preached with the flu, the stomach virus, even in an ice storm, in the drought, and no matter what, you knew where Joe Bob Boyd was on Sunday morning, Sunday night, and Wednesday night. Disciplined to work, disciplined to show up, disciplined to be up, and disciplined to stand up. You never wondered where Daddy stood on a matter. He was never on the fence, so to speak. He was disciplined to stand up, be up, show up.

Character trait nine: heroic. Daddy was our hero. Daddy was my hero. Daddy was Hannah's hero. Daddy was Jonah's hero. Daddy was Reagen's hero, and Henry's. He held us up when we couldn't hold ourselves. When Joe Bob got there, everyone would sigh in relief because we all knew it was going to be okay. "Joe Bob is here. Whew, thank goodness." Momma always said, "Everyone loves your daddy! Boy, they just can't wait for your daddy to get here." He was our hero, and I hope that he will always know this.

Often in a story, there is a point at which the character changes due to the plot. This happened on July 29, 2019. This character changed forevermore. That was how their story was written. Sometimes stories don't have happy endings, but the characters still can live happily ever after.

Our final trait of this character is lovable. I don't need to explain this to you. Daddy loved and loved and loved hard. He loved all his animals. A few years ago, he even had himself and Momma go down to the creek and dig up his first horse's, Paint's, bones and rebury them closer to his house. [laughter]

Momma said, "That's the craziest thing I've ever done! He had to make sure we got every bone!"

Daddy was nostalgic. He loved the simple things, and it is in that simplicity that everyone was attracted to him. In his simplicity he didn't like technology. He even considered a handheld lighter to light a candle, technology.

He said, "Everything should just be an on and off switch, simple. I don't like gadgets or buttons, just simple with a dial and on and off switch, no computers."

He did everything old school. Notebooks meticulously documented cattle, sermons, funerals and weddings and anything and everything. Daddy kept notes that would put the Pentagon to shame. As I was reading through some of these notes left from Daddy, I found this book that had not been completed the last time I looked, and I just happened to open it this week, and it was completed. And I'm going to close with one thing he wrote and then a poem that I've written.

Everything that you've heard out of my mouth at this podium has been written at my daddy's just this week. I found this book, and I opened it, and I couldn't believe he had completed it: "This is for Reagen, Jonah, and

Henry, a letter from your grandpa. Be a good girl and boy. Be a Christian in what you do. Stand for the truth. Help others. Be open, but always discerning. Don't give up after a defeat in life. Forgive and ask forgiveness. Oh, you know, all that good stuff that Christ would have in us. I love you, Bob."

This poem is titled "582-9307".

582-9307

Through the years of my life
In times of joy or strife,
I always had him to call
And let my burdens fall.

As early as I can remember
Be it spring, summer, fall, or winter,
I always had him to call
And let my burdens fall.

You see, Momma couldn't hear me.
Daddy would listen, and then she would see.
I always had him to call
And let my burdens fall.

This farmer's daughter and preacher's too,
What I needed he somehow always knew.
I always had him to call
And let my burdens fall.

From a little girl to who I am now,
We talked about God, Jesus, weather and cows.
I always had him to call
And let my burdens fall.

The number still remains,
But the location has changed.
582-9307
Now he isn't there,
He is in Heaven.

I always had him to call.
And let my burdens fall.

[Music]

PROUD TO BE A
PEANUT FARMER'S DAUGHTER

THERE IS A LITTLE spot on the map that has a big place in my heart. Nestled between Hillsboro and Whitney, just northwest of Peoria, is a community called Bethel. During childhood, many families move and live in many different places, but I only had this one. To say that stability was a staple in my life would be an understatement. We lived in a very simple, always pristine, but small country home on a hill inside a circle of tractors, farm equipment, cows, and sand—lots of sand.

My daddy was a farmer, and for over thirty years his primary crop was peanuts—Spanish reds, he would call them. In the fall, when I would be starting back to school, I remember riding the bus home and watching the dust follow like a billowing cloud of smoke, but once the dust settled, the smell of peanuts would sweeten the dry air.

I would go with my mom to sit in the truck, waiting on the tractor pulling the combine to fill up another trailer. Just because school was over for the day didn't mean that a farmer's work was too. Momma had books and magazines for us to read or draw in, but I never wanted to miss the action when the combine bucket was finally full, after what seemed like a million trips up and down the field rows, and about to pour thousands of those perfect peanuts into the trailer. My sister and I would always beg to play in the trailers, but Momma never wanted us to for fear of snakes or being buried alive in a sea of peanuts.

I can remember Daddy waving to us from the tractor with each pass and sometimes even blowing a kiss to Momma and me, feeling on top of the world as his little girl sitting in the bed of our old pickup or lying in the seat, waiting for another trailer to fill and another trip to the peanut house. We would go to the local peanut plant in Whitney to empty and leave the peanuts for drying, but tomorrow would be another day—up and down rows, filling and emptying trailers, and farming the many pieces of land my dad all called a different name (Griff, Sandpit, Archer, Rosenbaum, Pete Harris). I'm sure these names all had a meaning, but to me, they were just names, often written on small pieces of torn paper towel left on the kitchen counter to tell me my parents' location when I would get off the bus and walk to an empty house.

Spring, summer, and fall were hectic for farming families in the rural parts of Hill County, but no matter how busy my dad was in the field, he always had time for me, my sister, my momma, and others. Pastoring a church in Bethel for over thirty-three years, holding a community together while he held us, and making sure that my childhood was everything it needed to be made me who I am today. Through the years, seasons may come and go, but memories of tractors, trailers, sand, and combines will always make me proud to be a peanut farmer's daughter.

Written by Thelizabeth Boyd
Published Father's Day, June 14, 2019
Waxahachie Sun

RESOURCES

988 Suicide & Crisis Lifeline
1-800-273-8255

Call or text 988 or chat 988lifeline.org. The 988 Suicide & Crisis Lifeline is a national network of local crisis centers that provides free and confidential emotional support to people in suicidal crisis or emotional distress 24 hours a day, 7 days a week.

The current National Suicide Prevention Lifeline will remain available by calling 1-800-273-8255, but experts say the new three-digit code will be easier to remember during mental health emergencies.

Agricultural Stress and Suicide Helpline
833-897-2474

For anyone in the agriculture industry in need of support or help with mental health, the helpline number is 833-897-2474.

Crisis Text Line
Text MHA to 741741

Text MHA to 741741 and you'll be connected to a trained crisis counselor. Crisis Text Line provides free, text-based support 24/7.

Disaster Distress Helpline
1-800-985-5990

The national Disaster Distress Helpline is available for anyone experiencing emotional #distress related to natural or human-caused disasters. Call or text 1-800-985-5990 to be connected to a trained, caring counselor, 24/7/365. disasterdistress.samhsa.gov

Caregiver Help Desk
1-855-227-3640

Contact Caregiver Action Network's Care Support Team by dialing 855-227-3640. Staffed by caregiving experts, the Help Desk helps you find the right information you need to help you navigate your complex caregiving challenges. Caregiving experts are available 8:00 a.m.—7:00 p.m. ET.

The following list helped me. You can find it online at AARP.com; I shortened it for you below.

Two weeks after death:

- Secure certified copies of the death certificate
- Find the will and the executor
- Meet with a trusts and estates attorney
- Contact a CPA
- Take the will to probate
- Make an inventory of all assets
- Track down assets
- Make a list of bills
- Cancel services no longer needed

Notify the following of your loved one's death:

- Social Security Administration
- Life insurance companies
- Banks and other financial institutions
- Financial advisers and stockbrokers
- Credit agencies
- Cancel their driver's license
- Close credit card accounts
- Terminate insurance policies
- Delete or memorialize social media accounts
- Close email accounts
- Update voter registration

NO MORE SOMEDAY

WE ARE SAYING GOODBYE to another year soon and hello to a new start. A fresh calendar to mark up with schedules to keep and all those important things to do.

What about you?

Did you take a spot for yourself?

Is there something you have been putting off for someday in the future?

Too often we go about our daily craziness without a thought for what we may need to do for ourselves. We take time for work, school, necessary doctor appointments, and parties, but I urge you this year to look at something you have been putting off for yourself and write in on your calendar.

We hear ourselves say "someday," but I have yet to see this day listed on a calendar. Shockingly, there are seven days in a week, but no "Someday." For many, guilt sets in when we think of what we wanted as a child and where we are now. Life takes turns we do not expect, but that doesn't mean we can't turn the wheel.

I had many dreams growing up, and still do—attorney, public speaker, advocate, volunteer, counselor, nurse, wife, mother—I didn't grow up dreaming of being a teacher. I played teacher with my friends but never thought I would actually do it.

I am forty-six years old and a teacher, encompassing all those occupations listed above into one. Funny how life gives you what you wanted in a way you never thought possible. But I still have a few dreams hidden inside—just for me. There are two very important days in everyone's life—the day you were born and the day you realize why you were born.

I know I was put on this earth to write.

I started a book about my grandmother a few months ago. So I'll be writing "finish the book" on each day of my new calendar for 2019. Hopefully, a year from now, I will be finalizing the book.

What are you going to write on your new calendar?

Thelizabeth Boyd
Published December 18, 2018
Waxahachie Sun

Little did I know then that life would turn the wheel, and I would be writing a whole different book, a book on grief.

MOMMA'S RECIPES

Old-Fashioned Christmas Teacakes

1 cup shortening

1 cup sugar

2 eggs

1 tsp. baking powder

1 tsp. vanilla

3 cups all-purpose flour

Mix all ingredients (I like to use my hand-mixer), and when dough is stiff enough to handle, roll out to ¼-inch thickness. Cut with Christmas or round cookie cutters and decorate as desired. Place on a greased cookie sheet. Bake in a 350 degree F oven for about 15 minutes or until brown around the edges. (makes 3 dozen)

Chocolate-Covered Strawberries

1 to 2 qt. strawberries (I usually buy several, so I can pick out the best berries.)

2 (7 oz.) containers Baker's Dipping Chocolate

1 cup white chocolate chips

Rinse and dry the strawberries. While the strawberries are drying, prepare your baking sheet. Line with wax paper and spray with nonstick cooking spray.

Melt the chocolate in its container according to the directions on the package. Make sure strawberries are completely dry before dipping. Dip each strawberry up to its stem, making sure to completely cover each one. Lay on the prepared baking sheet.

When all the best strawberries have been dipped, place the cookie sheet in the refrigerator. Place white chocolate chips in a microwave-safe bowl and melt in the microwave. Using a sharp-tined fork, stir to get the consistency needed for drizzling. Take the strawberries out of the refrigerator, and using a back-and-forth motion with your fork, drizzle the white chocolate on your strawberries.

Beautiful!

Peanut Brittle

2 cups sugar

1 cup corn syrup

½ cup water

2½ cups raw peanuts

1 Tbsp. butter

1 tsp. vanilla

1 tsp. baking soda

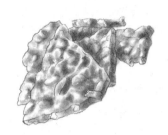

Cook the sugar, corn syrup, and water, stirring constantly, over medium heat until the mixture spins as a thread; then add the peanuts. Cook until golden brown. While continuing to stir, add the butter, vanilla, and baking soda. Mix and pour onto a large, buttered cookie sheet. Let the mixture cool and break into pieces. The colder the weather, the better! You can use larger cookie sheets to make a thinner brittle.

Creamy Banana Pudding

1 (14 oz.) can EAGLE BRAND®
Sweetened Condensed Milk

1½ cups cold water

1 (4-serving size) package instant
vanilla pudding mix

2 cups whipping cream,
whipped, or Cool Whip

1 large box of vanilla wafers

Lemon juice

3 medium bananas, sliced and dipped in lemon juice

In a large bowl, combine the sweetened condensed milk and water. Add the pudding mix; beat until well blended. Chill for 5 minutes.

Fold in the whipped cream. Spoon 1 cup of the pudding mixture into a 2½-quart glass serving bowl.

Top with one-third each of the vanilla wafers, bananas, and the remaining pudding mixture. Repeat the layers twice, ending with the pudding mixture. Chill thoroughly. Garnish as desired and serve. Store leftovers covered in the refrigerator.

Theo Boyd at her birthplace with a family photo, April 2022

50 SHADOWS

I WAS BORN IN A small Texas town called Whitney, on April 21, 1972, in a one-story, L-shaped building near the center of downtown. You may know it now as Urgent Care or Benji's, but it was once quite the busy hospital. I wasn't the only baby in the nursery, but I was the only one born on that day. *It was a Friday morning, 9:03 a.m., 7 pounds 12.5 ounces, 21.5 inches long* as Momma would remind me each year. Dr. Hill delivered me and would continue to be our doctor for years to come. You could say he is the first person I met in this town. I was a small shadow in his hands as he welcomed me and put me in Momma's arms for the first time.

The quiet streets that surround this place are filled with potholes and purpose. Every part of this town helped shape me in some way. Each shadow has a story behind it. Across from the hospital was the dentist where I got my first teeth cleaning. Next to that was the peanut house, where I watched Daddy empty full trailers of Spanish reds. Down the road a stretch, I started kindergarten with Mrs. Booth and Mrs. Penney, and each year I would return to a new grade with a new teacher who influenced my life somehow. I have Wildcat blood flowing inside, pushing me to give back some of what I was given.

From the first cry I made inside this hospital to the Friday night "Go Wildcats!" yell at Baker Field, I still have a voice. From my first steps to marching in white boots in front of this building for a homecoming parade, I am still moving forward. No matter what direction we go in life, our shadow is there following us and reminding us of who we are.

Being my parents' first child, I didn't lack attention. Each year, Momma would decorate the kitchen and dining room with streamers, balloons, a gift, and a homemade cake. I don't remember any of the gifts, but I do remember the pink streamers and balloons that were so beautifully strung along the ceiling. Oh, and I always remember the cakes!

I find it hard to believe I'm no longer that little girl, waking up to pink streamers and balloons with the smell of cake baking in the oven. I still have birthdays, but they aren't as special as the ones when I lived back home. I grew up. I moved away, shadows and all.

As I approach a milestone birthday, I see fifty shadows, pushing me up and ready to hold me if I fall. Each year, I add another number to my age, and another shadow lines up behind me. My shadows have been there the entire time. As I look back, I can see some of them so clearly.

I see my shadow rocking in my mother's arms.

I see my shadow sitting on top of Daddy's shoulders.

I see my shadow carrying a watermelon
or bending down to feed a baby calf.

I see my shadow swinging on the playground.

I see my shadow baptized with hands folded to pray.

I see my shadow at the piano playing its keys.

I see my shadow with my hand stretched out to marry.

I see my shadow with my stomach big and
round, holding my daughter inside.

I see my shadow holding my daughter's hand.

I see my shadow alone, watching
him leave me for another.

I see my shadow bending down to
hug my mother's grave.

I see my shadow bending down to
hug my daddy's lifeless body.

I see my shadow watching everything leave.

I see my shadow rising to stand another day.

The shadows may have taken different shape through the years, but they are all mine. A heart may break, but the shadow never shows the cracks or breaks inside. No matter what changes happen in our life, we are still whole. The shadow remains solid and full, holding us when we can't hold ourselves.

I know that every part of who I am is because of where I came from. I may have fifty shadows, but there is only one me. Maybe it's time I let my shadows lead the way.

NOTES